HIS PURPOSE
FOR ME

To Virginia & Darlene,
Thanks for showing an interest
in my story.
May my book be both a
blessing and an inspiration to you.
Please share it with family
and friends.
Best Regards,
Gene

ACTS 4:12

HIS PURPOSE
FOR ME

A STORY OF ADOPTION, ABUSE, RECOVERY,
SALVATION, BLESSING AND REUNION

GENE LING

Pleasant W rd

Pleasant Word (a division of WinePress Publishing, PO Box 428, Enumclaw, WA 98022) functions only as book publisher. As such, the ultimate design, content, editorial accuracy, and views expressed or implied in this work are those of the author.

ISBN 1-4141-0726-9
Library of Congress Catalog Card Number: 2006902242

Though the Lord is on high, he looks upon the lowly, but the proud he knows from afar.

Though I walk in the midst of trouble, you preserve my life; you stretch out your hand against the anger of my foes, with your right hand you save me.

The Lord will fulfill His Purpose for Me; your love, O Lord, endures forever—do not abandon the works of your hands. Psalm 138:6-8 The Holy Bible (NIV)

DEDICATION

This work is dedicated to my very special sister, Judy, my twin.

This is a story about *Adoption, Abuse, Recovery, Salvation, Blessing,* and *Reunion;* with both adoptive and biological family.

It is the story of God's providential hand in my life; not always seen, but always there.

It is my story, written in my own words.

Gene Ling

CLARIFICATION

As I begin writing this narrative I see a need for some clarification. Most people have had only one mother. Judy, my twin sister, and I have had four "mothers."

It will be necessary to distinguish them from each other in order to make this story flow smoothly and avoid confusion to the reader. With this in mind, the distinctions are as follows:

"Mother"—will always refer to our BIRTH mother, Dora Killen Brinton Hall.

"Mom"—will always refer to our ADOPTIVE mother, Betty Taylor Ling.

"Mom-mom"—refers to our ADOPTIVE grandmother, (Dad's mother), Irene Beeson Ling Tunison.

"Agnes"—refers to our STEPMOTHER, Agnes Currier Mc-Ferren Ling (Dad's wife after divorcing "Mom.")

ACKNOWLEDGEMENTS

First and foremost I wish to thank my sister Judy for the contributions of her recollections of our individual and combined personal histories to this book. Her input has been invaluable to the success of my manuscript.

Secondly, I am extremely grateful to the continued support of my family, especially my wife; Carol's relentless and faithful encouragement has been the motivation that has kept me committed to this project.

Also, I wish to express my thanks to my pastor, the Rev. Matt Mancini, for his appreciation for what it was I wanted to do, and the guidance to get me started.

And finally, a very special thanks to Dr. Thom Scott; and Richard and Susan Graves, whose expertise in literary and computer matters contributed immensely to the preparation of my manuscript.

My sincere and heartfelt thanks to all.

ABOUT MY WRITING

It is sometimes said by those who reside in the United Kingdom that the people of the United States do not speak English, they speak *American!*

That statement is probably very true; we Americans don't always use proper English when expressing ourselves. We tend to be more concerned with just getting our message across, and making sure that we do, without regards to whether we are precisely accurate in our speech.

Having said that; I expect to endure some criticism about the *style* in which I have used in expressing myself in writing this story. I do not claim to have always been without literary errors in putting my story down on paper; but then, neither am I overly concerned about it.

I could have, of course, avoided all such concerns by having this work go through the traditional editing process; and I have been encouraged by many to do so.

I have declined to do that.

The reason for this is simple. When I embarked on this project, I approached it from the idea that I was telling my story to a *single* individual, one-on-one. I have written the entire narrative tuned to the idea that I have had a person sitting across a table from me while I was telling it; speaking to that particular individual in *"American."*

And, as I have already stated, this is *my* story, *written in my own words;* and so it must be.

For this reason, it is extremely important *to me* that it be written as *I* would tell it, and not an editor.

TABLE OF CONTENTS

"WHERE'S MOMMY?"

BIRTH, DEATH, AND ADOPTION

What is the earliest memory that you have of your childhood?" That is a question that most people have had posed to them at one time or another.

For me, it was standing in the driveway of the house at 618 Summit Avenue in Prospect Park, Pennsylvania. This is the house that we would live in for the next nine years or so. We were moving. "We," meaning our adoptive father, Bill Ling, my twin sister Judy, and me.

Dad and his wife Betty, our adoptive mom, were separating and would eventually divorce. Of course Judy and I had no knowledge of this; nor would we have any understanding of what was going on anyhow. We were just five years old and the words adoption, separation, and divorce would not have had any meaning to us at the time. That would come much later. Abuse was another word and practice that we didn't know about, however, we were to find out its full meaning in the years to come. It would also become the primary reason Betty left the marriage. Judy and I are still at a loss as to why mom did not take us with her, but perhaps she knew that she wouldn't have the means to properly take care of us.

We were moving from our home on 9th Ave., just three blocks away, to our "new" home which belonged to dad's mother; now divorced from his father and remarried. The neighborhood knew them as Irene and Daniel (Doc) Tunison, but Judy and I would know them as "Mom-mom" and "Pop-pop," our adoptive grandparents.

The year was 1945 and World War II was still in progress, although no one could know that it was winding down. Nazi Germany was all but defeated and would surrender in May. And even as the war was still raging in the Pacific, the bombing of Nagasaki and Hiroshima in August would hasten the demise of the Japanese Empire.

I do not remember very much about our move, and what I do remember is somewhat sketchy, given our age, but there are a few things that remain in my memory.

The move was certainly in the early spring or summer. I know this because I can still recall that the day was warm and I was wearing little brown shorts. It's strange, but I do not remember Judy being there, but I know that she was. I do remember dad and Mom-mom seemed sad and a little angry and, of course, I did not know why.

Pop-pop was nowhere to be found and was most likely at work. He was employed by the Chester Brewery Co., in Chester, Pa. as a bookkeeper. His future there would be limited though, along with his fellow employees, as the brewery would close in 1953.

Judy can remember that at some point during the move walking with dad the three blocks from the old home to the new. She distinctly recalls pushing her baby carriage loaded with the many dolls she had. Her memory is that it was a nice balmy day and that it was most likely in early spring.

As I stood there in the driveway there was one other thing that I had noticed. There was a woman sitting on the front steps of her house directly across from Mom-mom's.

She was occupied between watching our move and her two small boys playing in their front yard. These were the Fries, a first- generation Irish couple that immigrated here in the late1920's. Michael and Kathleen had met as employees of a wealthy family in the Philadelphia area; she being the housekeeper and cook, and he the family's chauffeur.

At this point in 1945 they had four children; Michael, Patrick, Mary, and Tommy. And in the very near future there would be a fifth child, Billy Fries.

A tragic incident in years to come involving Billy would have a tremendous impact on my life; especially in regards to my views concerning life, death, and God. But for now my focus was on the two boys in the yard, Michael and Patrick.

Mike was one year my senior and Pat was a year younger than me. We would become childhood friends, inseparable; a friendship that would last throughout our formative years and well into high school.

The thing that I can remember about this incident is that at some point Mrs. Fries "caught my eye" and gave me a smile and a small wave with her hand. I remember very sheepishly returning the gesture and then turning away, transferring my attention back to what was going on with the move.

Then at some point during this day I realized that "mommy" was nowhere to be found. I can vividly recall asking the obvious question, "Where's mommy?" I can also vaguely remember feeling that I had done something wrong in just asking it. I received a blank and somewhat angry look from both dad and Mom-mom but no verbal reply.

The feeling that I should not have asked would be supported by future responses to our inquiries about our mom. In future years we would be rebuked for asking by such replies as, "Keep your damn mouth shut, it's none of your business!" There were a few occasions when such a question would earn me a sharp slap across the mouth, and always from the hand of Mom-mom.

It became evident in years to come that we were not going to get any information as to what had transpired, or as to where our mom was located. It also would become clear in the future that the family's intention was that we would never see her again.

But they were wrong.

God would overrule them; and in His providential timing we would be reunited once again.

That event would unfold 56 years later.

> There is no wisdom, no insight, no plan that can succeed against the Lord.
>
> —Proverbs 21:30 (NIV)

Since Judy and I are twins, I used to refer to us as former "womb-mates." I entered into this life a full one-and-a-half minutes before my sister. This, I claim, has always given me the right to the position of being her "older" brother. I have jokingly reminded her of this, and I have insisted that she revere and offer me the respect that is rightfully mine; having the profound wisdom of an elder brother. Of course, I don't know how much worldly wisdom is attained in under two minutes, but it is a status that I have refused to relinquish.

And then there is her rebuttal; which is that the only reason I was first was because it was too crowded "in there" and she kicked me out! It is something that we have had fun bantering back and forth about over the years.

We were born on January 16, 1940 at Crozer Hospital in Upland, Pa. The site was also generally known as the Crozer Home for Incurables and Homeopathic Hospital. It is my understanding that "incurables" usually referred to those suffering from cancer, tuberculosis, and other such diseases which, at that time, were all but considered a "death sentence."

The best that we can tell, our home was at 515 E. 7th Street in Chester. This is the address given on our mother's death certificate and is where we most likely resided at the time.

She died when we were just a little over two years old, on February 3, 1942; just two days before her thirty-first birthday. The cause of death was double pneumonia, and she had been a patient at Fitzgerald Mercy Hospital in Darby, Pa. for twenty-two days; which leaves us to believe that she had been ill for some time. She has been described by family members as frail and sickly, and we had envisioned her as being a small, petite woman. However, photos obtained from family members in recent years belie that image.

Judy's name given at birth was Judith Lee Hall and mine was Eugene Carroll Hall, Jr., obviously named after our father. Our mother's name was Dora Killen Brinton Hall. Killen being her maiden name, the family was very well known in the Aston Township area.

William Killen, our grandfather, was a multi-talented attraction of a fifteen member minstrel group that performed regularly in the Philadelphia, Camden, N.J., and Wilmington, DE. areas as well as Aston. He was very much involved in local politics and there is an American Legion Post named after his brother James who was killed in World War I.

The Killen name would also become familiar with most of the residents of Delaware County during the year of 1928. Our mother at the time was engaged to a Norman "Tubby" Gibson. Her fiancé was robbed and murdered just two weeks before they were to be married and the story was front page news in The Chester Times, which was the primary newspaper for the county.

A murder was big news in those days; and the event, the investigation, capture, and ensuing trial of those responsible would be the "lead" story, having been given a prominent place on page one. I have been able to obtain copies of the eleven consecutive days of front page coverage of those events.

Dora's first marriage was to one Paul Brinton. The Brinton name was another well established family in the area, not only in Aston Township but throughout all of Delaware County. They were very early settlers in the region, and the family's history has been the subject of several books; and to this day the Brinton homestead in Chadds Ford continues to delight tourists.

Dora and Paul's marriage produced two children, Paul Jr. and Barbara. That marriage would be short-lived though, due mainly to Paul's heavy drinking. It would seem that divorce is one common thread that runs throughout our family's history.

We have obtained a fair amount of information about our mother from family members that we have been re-united with in recent years. Our father, however, remains somewhat a mystery. We know very little about him and our research continues.

It is our grandmother Killen's signature on our mother's death certificate, identifying and claiming her body, and not Eugene Hall's. The whereabouts of our father at the time of our mother's death is unknown.

However, his signature does appear on the adoption decree and clearly states that he was present during the proceedings. The court papers state that the decree was awarded on April 20, 1942; just a little over two-and-a half months after our mother's death. For an adoption decree to be awarded in less than six months in the state of Pennsylvania is regarded as highly unusual. It has been suggested that there had to be some unusual circumstances, and *influence*, for this to have happened.

That's where Mom-mom comes in.

Irene Beeson Ling Tunison was born in Chelsea, Aston Township on February 6, 1892. She attended school in West Chester, and upon graduation continued her education at Banks Business College. This gave her a tremendous advantage for employment in the business world, since higher education for women at the time was not the norm.

She started her work history as a court recorder; working at the Media Courthouse, the County seat for Delaware

County. In time, opportunities moved her forward and she was eventually appointed personal secretary to Judge Sweeny, the president judge and top judicial figure for the county. By the time the three of us were moving to live with her and Pop-pop, she would be working as secretary for the Delaware County District Attorney William McClenahan, Jr. Ironically, Mr. McClenahan had been the prosecuting attorney in the "Tubby" Gibson murder trial.

It is generally believed by family members that her influence and connections expedited the adoption process. This assumption is further supported by the records I have obtained from the Orphans Court. One Tamica Wayne works for the court and has assisted me with court petitions in my information quest. She has strongly suggested the two families involved knew each other as there are no records of an intermediary adoption agency being included in the proceedings.

In addition, our Aunt Bernice, Bill Ling's sister, has repeatedly stated that our grand- mother was terrified at the thought of her son being actively involved in the war and the adoption would change his draft status. She believes that Mom-mom "pushed" for the adoption process to move forward quickly before Bill would have to face the first round of the draft; that being married men without children.

It was a strong relationship; and in time it would become apparent just how strong that mother-son relationship would be.

"But you, O God, do see trouble and grief; you consider it to take it in hand. The victim commits himself to you; you are the helper of the fatherless.

—Psalm 10:14 (NIV)

CHAPTER TWO

618 SUMMIT AVENUE (THE YOUNG YEARS)

Like most people, my recollections of my very early years are, at most, fragmentary; a hodge-podge of memories seemingly without any kind of chronological order. The same could be said of Judy; she also admits that there doesn't seem to be any real continuity to her remembrance of those early times growing up together. However, we have very much enjoyed, for the most part, "picking each other's brain" to see just what we do remember, focusing on only the good times we had together. We don't need to be reminded of the bad.

One might say that our individual input into these conversations could be partitioned off into three categories. The first would be what we very vividly remember together, mutually agreeing as to how those events played out. The second is somewhat similar, although we might disagree on some of the fine points; one of those, "That's not quite exactly how I remember it!" type situations. Of course, any one of those particular memories could just be a matter of our own personal interpretation, a difference in how we each mentally processed the information at the time.

The third category has been the most fun. Those memories that either of us had long ago since forgotten; brought to the surface once again after having been buried under the layers of time. Sometimes tweaking those memories would produce others, and after awhile it could be amazing just how much we would recall about those years.

In this segment, the separate and collective memories I would like to share has been specifically limited to our nine years living with our adoptive grandparents; at a later time in my story I will include comments dealing with the contrasts of home life after "dad" built his home and we went to live with him.

I Remember!

It was my first experience with "recycling."

It was the war years, and even at age five I had to "contribute" to the war effort. It was my job to squash flat whatever *tin cans* we had, to be placed out by the curb once a week for pickup. Most of our nation's tin was imported from South America, and the concern over the German U-boat "wolf packs" operating off our Atlantic coast was a continual worry. I can remember "dad" saying that he and some friends would travel over to Cape May, New Jersey at night to "view the sights." They could witness the glow on the horizon caused by the burning of the ships torpedoed by the Germans, and on a few occasions they could detect the low rumbling of the explosions that precipitated those flames.

Anything rubber was collected! Car and bicycle tires, inner tubes, raincoats, and rubber boots. Again, one could look up and down the street and see piles of these items stacked for pickup.

There were nighttime blackout drills, with planes (ours) flying over the neighborhoods to make sure the residents had no light emitting from their homes. It was a time when families purchased heavy black curtains to place over their windows during these "raids"; and there were Civil Patrol authorities roaming the streets, ready to fine any household that failed to comply.

And, gasoline, sugar, and meat were all rationed. I'm sure there were other items that required their availability to be controlled, but these are the ones I remember. The house that was our grandparents was heated by a huge coal furnace, with a very large coal bin at the bottom of the basement steps. In a few years they would switch to oil for heat, but in those first early years it was the burning of coal that kept us warm in the wintertime.

I remember the coal deliveries; the big trucks stacked with large canvas bags filled with that shiny black product piled high on the flatbed. The driver, and apparent supervisor, was usually white, and the laborers who did all the "bull-work" were always black men, a somewhat racist practice very typical for the times.

I was always impressed by the obvious strength of these men, slinging those heavy bags with their contents over their shoulders, and transporting them to the chute through the basement window to replenish our supply in the bin. I imagined that these men had to be incredibly tired after such a hard days work.

Mom-mom was still working at the courthouse when we first moved in, Pop-pop was at the brewery in Chester; and of course, dad was also employed; although I am unsure as to where. He changed jobs often during these early years, and I don't recall exactly where he worked; except for one. His occupation at one point was driving a truck as a deliveryman for the Hires Company. I remember this

31

because every Friday he would bring home a case of root beer, something Judy and I looked forward to.

Since all the adults in the household would be gone each day during the work week, it was necessary to find someone to look after Judy and I during their absence.

Mom-mom absolutely *hated* housework, which, coupled with the need for supervision for Judy and me, hired a black domestic by the name of Nettie to fulfill these responsibilities. She did the cleaning, the ironing, and the babysitting.

Now; I had a very extensive supply of wooden building blocks which I would use to construct various castles, buildings, and garages, as any young boy would be apt to do.

One day, for whatever reason, Judy and I were sitting on the floor at opposite ends of the dining room table. While playing with these blocks, I got the uncontrollable urge to toss one over the table in Judy's direction. She threw it back. We escalated the action into a true block fight! Unfortunately, we either didn't notice, or we ignored, Mom-mom's fine dining room chandelier over the center of the table. Smash, smash, smash!!

To this day Judy claims that she can still visualize the holes we created in the globes encompassing the light bulbs. Nettie came quickly to the dining room to see what all the "tinkling" of glass was about, and was duly alarmed. I still don't know how she was able to explain to our grandmother the damage done by us, but she must have done an excellent job because Judy and I suffered no discipline for that incident.

Mom-mom was good to Nettie. She treated this black woman with true dignity, and more as a friend than an employee.

In a few years Mom-mom would quit the courthouse, and she and Pop-pop would purchase the corner store up the street from the house and rename it "Tunison's Market." The local "mom and pop" grocery stores were the norm back then, long before the supermarket chains captured the market; no pun intended!

What we both remember about the few remaining years that Nettie would be our unofficial "nanny"; to begin for us what would be a period of time when Judy and I would be left alone to fend for ourselves, was that Mom-mom insisted that Nettie take a true lunch break.

Our grandmother would come down from the store every afternoon and require Nettie to sit down at the kitchen table while she prepared her lunch, and it was always a cooked meal. I think our grandmother truly enjoyed this diligent, hardworking black woman's company; in addition to taking care of our home while Mom-mom focused most of her valuable time on running the family business. And, as far as being our babysitter, Judy and I would agree that it was Nettie who probably spent more time overseeing our activities during that time than there ever was to be in the next five years to come. We had very little, if any, supervision during those last years we were to live with our grandparents. In today's society and culture it would very easily be considered neglect, and perhaps foster charges of child endangerment. Especially had any of our shenanigans produced any serious results, and the potential was there.

Nettie never worked on weekends, and since Mom-mom and Pop-pop were preoccupied with the store, Judy and I had to fend for ourselves. Dad? He was never around.

We also had to entertain ourselves.

There were two independent frequent rituals (at about age eight), which actually became common practices that both of us can recall which could have had disastrous results. One involved Judy and me, and the other dangerous episodes were solely mine.

Together, we made "forts" under a table in the basement. We used extra blankets for the sides and "flooring." We would then collect our comic books, some snacks for a treat, and a half dozen or so *candles!* We had five or six large candles burning at any one time, and it's a wonder we didn't set ourselves on fire, burn down the house, *or both!*

My solo dangerous antic was symbolically a result of the victorious allied armies of World War II. Toy soldiers were a very popular item for the male children at the time and I had more than my share. I had lots of them, and I and my childhood friends would play "war" in my grandmothers front yard. Sometimes a few of my soldiers would get lost, only to be found at a later time decapitated by the family lawnmower.

One of the weapons used during the actual historical war that intrigued me was the flamethrower. On thinking about that lethal instrument used in combat, I decided to try and create my own. Our grandfather was a smoker of cigars and had a few lighters placed around the house. Lighters don't work without lighter fluid.

I "borrowed" a can of lighter fluid; got some blue-tipped wooden matches from the kitchen cabinet and returned to the "battlefield." There I would remove the cap to the can, set the tip of the can on fire with the matches, and press on the can to create a fine stream of flame. I would *always* be lying on the ground on my stomach while doing this. Later on I would shudder at the thought of that can of flammable fluid exploding in my face.

There is a saying that says, "The Lord looks after fools and drunks"; and…well, I was much too young to drink! That would come later.

While I was outside burning up our grandparent's front yard, Judy would be "teaching" school on our enclosed front porch; with the younger neighborhood kids for her "students." I'm still at a loss as to why these kids enjoyed it so much, didn't they have enough of it through the week?

We were almost *totally* on our own at about age nine. We were left alone for most of the time after school, and the weekend time always seemed to be exclusively ours. The only real rule we had was to make sure we were home in the evening before it got too dark; the turning on of the street lights being our signal. Judy has reminded me of this, saying, "We literally ran the streets and were on our own until dark; we always had to be home at dark." Other than that we were pretty much without adult contact most of the day; and there was very little, if any, structure to our lives.

For the most part it was our responsibility to feed ourselves at breakfast and lunch. Breakfast was always cereal until Mom-mom taught us how to cook eggs, at about age eleven; and once taught we would then left alone, unsupervised, to do our own cooking; something else that would not be permitted today.

Dinner was *always* a toss-up, "catch as catch can", whenever Mom-mom would come down from the store to prepare it. That could be anywhere from 5 to 9 pm.

Judy and I were very close during those early years; and as she would say, "We were *always* together; we had our arguments, but we were still always there for each other." I think we were unwittingly each others support and company. And, I constantly thank our Lord that He kept us together; that we had not been separated and been adopted by two different families. We probably would have never found each other.

She remembers us walking together the six blocks or so to school all bundled up in our snow suits. Hers was rose-colored, and mine was blue, all one piece with a belt in the middle. The policeman (no crossing guards then) on the

35

corner always looked for us and called us "Billy Bundles." Why he did that, who can say? He may have known "dad" and his label for us was a variation of "Bill's Bundles."

Television was a new invention at that time and not as yet generally available, or for most families, affordable. I think we ended up being the third family on the street to buy one. It was a true novelty when they first came out, and any family that had one shared it with multiple families from the neighborhood. It was not at all unusual for people to open their doors to allow others to check out this fantastic 12 inch, round, black and white viewing contraption with almost perfect strangers. Besides, there was a particular amount of pride involved in owning one, and gave, a least for a brief period of time, a family a certain level of 'status'.

Until then, however, radio, movie theatres, and creating our own entertainment is how we spent our free time.

Radio was the mainstay of any family's entertainment and every household had one, just as a television is commonplace in every home today. It was where one found the news of the day, listened to their favorite sports events, and the weekly radio programs that entailed engaging our imagination to create our own images as to what we were listening to over the airwaves.

Judy and I would sit together behind a large chair in our grandparent's living room, ears glued to the radio so we wouldn't miss any word or sound effects that were part of our favorite shows, and there were many.

The comedy programs "Baby Snooks" starring Fanny Bryce, and "The Life of Riley", were two of our favorites. I can still picture myself rolling around on the floor, laughing hysterically at the character known as, "Digger O' Dell, the friendly undertaker" from the "Riley" show. His voice characterization alone would be enough to get me started.

Then there were the crime and mystery programs; The Green Hornet, The Fat Man, and The Shadow. And I rarely missed an episode of my two favorites, Superman and The Lone Ranger. Ah! They were much simpler times, and in some very special ways, the *"good old days"*, apart from our family life of course.

Saturday afternoons almost always entailed our weekly visit to "The Manor Theatre", the local movie house in Prospect Park. I can recall Mom-mom giving each of us two dimes; *fifteen cents for admission, and a nickel for a box of candy!* Wow! Talk about inflation!

These matinees consisted of twenty-five "Looney Tunes" cartoons, and a serial or two; usually Buck Rodgers or, of course, The Lone Ranger. The continuation of the story prompted one to make every effort to return the next week.

Unless the weather was unusually bad, rain or snow, we were always outside. There was no isolation of individuals due to " *progress*"; no inundating of electronic games or computers to undermine our socializing.

Communities were very close-knit during those times and everybody knew everyone who was their neighbor on any given street. Very, very, rarely did any family move. I can remember only one "For Sale" sign going up on our street the whole time we grew up. Families were not near as mobile back then as they are today.

All us kids knew each other, from blocks away; and whenever we would get together for a game of any kind, anyone who wanted to play was included. No one was re-fused participation.

Some of the games we played were, "Kick the can", "Hide and Seek", "Simon Says", "Kickball", and of course, baseball. The only criteria for participation was that one had to be old enough to have permission from their parents to play in the street. That was it; the only stipulation!

One of our most popular games was "Prisoner of War", a variation of "Hide and Seek", and the shed under our grandparents back porch was the "stockade."

With so many kids involved in these games the noise we created could be quite loud. It always brings to mind one comical incident involving the Fries family.

Our childhood friends and neighbors from across the street, Mary, Tommy, Mike, and Pat Fries were all involved in playing a game of "kick the can" with the rest of us kids, probably numbering a dozen players. Mike, Pat, and Tommy were having a boisterous argument over one of the fine points of the game. Poor Mary hadn't said a word, but the argument was so loud that in a few minutes time Mr. Fries, their father, came out and demanded, "What the hell is all the yelling about?"; being somewhat vocal himself! "Get in the house, right now, all of you!" Mary tried to plead her case, saying; "But dad, I didn't do anything, I haven't said a word"; but to no avail. Undaunted, immediately Mr. Fries' response, laced with typical Irish blarney and humor was, "Ah, that's the trouble with 'ya girl, you're too damn quiet; in the house with ya now, 'til ya learn to be more sociable". .... I must have laughed for a good ten minutes!

These are the good memories Judy and I have of the years living on Summit Avenue, a definitive contrast to the indifference, neglect, and abuse we also experienced. Our grandparents preoccupation and time was with their store, and our "father" was seldom around to foster any real relationship between us. He was, for all practical purposes, a father *in absentia.*

Almost all the recollections of any good times we had as children involves our interaction with each other as brother and sister, or of course, our friends from the neighborhood; I honestly and objectively cannot remember <u>a single instance</u> when it included our "family." Judy has also repeatedly confirmed that claim.

My sister and I found our companionship and support in each other, and there is no question in my mind that the Lord had His protective hand upon us during these all important formative years.

> Though my father and mother forsake me, The Lord will receive me.
>
> —Psalm 27:10 (NIV)

WHO WOULD I BE?

For my sister, Judy.

Who would I be, If I wasn't me?
Our mother's love lost before we were three.
Cast away branches, you and me.
Cast away branches from our father's tree.
And who would I be, If I wasn't me?
Tossed to a family by a court's decree.
Our future, our welfare; not an issue, you see.
We were just two needed pieces; two pawns in their game.
With deceit and lies abounding; just adding to their shame.
And if things had been different; would we be the same?
Had known another family; worn a different last name.
Our memories would have been altered; that is certainly true.
Would that have changed who we are, me and you?
It's a question never to be answered; a forever mystery.
Still, I wonder who I might be; if I wasn't me.
Fond memories of our childhood? No, there is none to be
found there.
Was there anyone interested, did anyone care?
And as I ponder these questions; entertained just for awhile.
The thoughts bring forth a brief grin; then transforms into a
smile.
For I know that who we are; was designed from above.
With God's protection upon us; and His immeasurable love.
So, we are the persons that we are supposed to be.
But, just for a moment; I still wonder, you see.
Who would I be; if I wasn't me?
Gene Ling

CHAPTER THREE

THE WALTSONS
AND
MCFERRENS

What Judy and I know about the background of the Waltson family is scattered, due mainly because of a lack of interest on our part. At our young age we just didn't seem to place any importance on knowing a lot about it, probably because we were preoccupied with other questions we were trying to have answered.

Neither of us can recall the exact birth date of our aunt, although we both agree it was sometime in May of 1915. We know that our adoptive father was born in 1913 and he was two years older than her.

Also, the exact year of her marriage to our Uncle Bert is uncertain; but we put it at 1938 or 1939, since their son, our cousin Kenny, was just a year older than Judy and I.

The family was greatly opposed to the marriage, mainly because of the fact that Bert Waltson was Jewish. It was a time in our culture when prejudices towards other racial and ethnic backgrounds were more blatantly open and commonplace than they are today. However, the attitude of objection to the marriage was likewise reciprocated by the Waltson family, they were very much opposed to Bert marrying a non-Jew.

Irrespective of their individual family's wishes, they followed their hearts and married anyway. It would eventually turn out to be the right decision; they have had, unquestionably, the best marriage than any other, on *either* side of the families!

Joan would be the next addition to the Waltson family. "Joanie", as Judy and I would nickname her, was a year younger than us, and she rounded out what I would eventually refer to as, "the fabulous four."

There would still be one more child for Aunt Bernice and Uncle Bert, and that was their other daughter Nancy. She would arrive much later in the marriage, what Judy would describe as a "change of life baby." Because of the disparity in our ages, our relationship with her never really developed, however, with Kenny and Joan it was an entirely different story.

We truly enjoyed being together, and always looked forward to an occasion when we could be. They would visit with us at Mom-mom's house fairly frequently during these very early stages of our childhood, and we would be involved in playing card games, Monopoly, drawing, and going to the Manor movies together.

I can still chuckle at the memory of the time when Kenny and I decided to combine our artistic "ability" and create our own funds for our excursions to the movie theatre. With great diligence and concentration we embarked on a project of counterfeiting our own one-dollar bills. We must have been all of ten or eleven years of age, each with a crisp new dollar bill in front of us to ensure the accuracy of our endeavor. Naturally, it didn't take us long to realize just how difficult and hopeless our efforts were. They were so lacking in the representation of the real thing that I can never remember ever again trying to artfully copy *anything!* Anyhow, it has been a true memory maker, *for sure!*

Most of the time we would spend together was at the cottage located at Crystal Beach, Maryland. Each year the four of us would be with our grandparents for several trips there in the early Spring and Fall; left to ourselves to "explore" the entire area on our own. We would be gone all day long, without any overseer's to our activities. In addition to this, Mom-mom and Pop-pop always seem to fit in annual day trips to Wildwood, New Jersey; where the four of us could be found body-surfing in the ocean and roaming the boardwalk, trying to decide which amusement rides we wanted to try.

Coupled with the holiday dinners, and the frequent visits of our cousins to Summit Avenue, we ended up spending a considerable amount of time with each other. This was particularly true after our aunt and uncle built their own cabin at the beach in Maryland. They would traditionally reside there throughout the summer, and when Judy and I spent our two weeks vacation at the cottage of our grandparents, we could always be found together. This lasted well into our early teen years, and then our individual attentions were slowly being channeled to other interests, usually involving members of the opposite sex.

These were the times my sister and I found to be a stabilizing factor, a reprieve from the discord and turmoil of the home life that was all too familiar. Without a doubt, whenever Judy and I reminisce about our childhood we always, *without exception*, recall the good times with our cousins, Kenny and Joan; "the fabulous four."

The next thing that is absolutely imperative that I mention is about my aunt Bernice. I cannot emphasize enough the influence she had on me in retaining some measure of self- esteem. She was *the only* adult in my entire childhood that I can remember having given me any measure of emotional acceptance and support.

She always had a kind word for me, *always* seemed to be genuinely glad to see me on every occasion, and <u>the only one</u> who might praise me for anything! Not until many years later would I understand the reason behind it; and the *why* will be revealed later on in my story.

In later years, it would be our aunt Bernice who would give Judy and I a true picture of who Bill Ling *really* was. I don't think it was their obvious ongoing animosity towards each other that precipitated her comments; I think it was more of an attempt to accurately describe a personal side of our "father" we were totally unaware of. Judy and I both had our suspicions, but it was our aunt Bernice who would give credibility to them. However, there was never a deliberate act on her part to undermine his image, which would be totally out of character for her; neither of us can remember our aunt maliciously gossiping about anyone. That simply was *not* our aunt Bernice; her speech was what we Christians would describe as being sprinkled with "grace"; she rarely had an unkind word to say. She was simply confirming what we had already suspected.

Bill Ling was to eventually earn for himself the description, and reputation as a true "playboy." He rarely worked in his early adult life, lived with his mother; and, according to our aunt Bernice, was every bit "the ladies man."

He was a very sharp dresser, which in time would earn him the nickname "Dapper- Dan." He always seemed to have plenty of money (where did he get it?), and was a known gambler. He once put up his car as a bet in a poker game, and lost! Not to worry; his *mother* bought him another one.

It is my impression he again briefly pursued that lifestyle after our mom and he divorced; for Judy and I rarely saw him in the evenings at home. Even after he remarried we were seldom together, he living in an apartment with his new wife and her daughter.

Judy would say, "The only time we see him is when we've misbehaved, or it's "report card" time, or on holidays. Our situation was never conducive to establishing a true relationship with our "father."

Agnes McFerren and Bill were married in April of 1948. He and his new wife and her daughter Joan from her previous marriage moved into one of the two apartments over the building that was Tunison's Market and the Laundromat; and to this day I have my suspicions as to whether he ever paid any rent to his mother for the accommodations.

The apartment was relatively small, a two bedroom, which necessitated that Judy and I remain living with our grandparents.

This arrangement contributed to perpetuating and expanding the alienation between our "father" with Judy and I. Judy still refers to him as "Bill", refusing to attach the label of "dad" or "father" to him. In her eyes he was only our father in the legal sense, nothing more. She is not at all wrong.

So many times as a young boy I longed to interact with him, only to be left disappointed. On reflection, it gives credibility to the belief that she and I were just "used", adopted only to serve a particular selfish need on their part.

I can recall so many times when he would come home from work and "check in" with his mother *every day,* walking down to the house before ever first seeing his wife. Invariably he would pass me while I was playing in the front yard, or in the street in front of our grandparents house where Judy and I continued to live. He *never* spoke to me; he would look in my direction but never speak, no "hello", *nothing!*

One particular incident that vividly sticks in my mind even to this day is when he had called down to the house on the telephone and asked for me. I can still remember him saying to me, "Come on up to the apartment, I want to see you."

I ran up the street with anticipation, thinking, "Oh Boy! Daddy and I are going to do something!" I burst through the door to the apartment, not bothering to close it, and ran up the long flight of steps to the second floor, excited! He was waiting for me at the top.

With a grin on his face he said to me, "Here's a nickel; go over to the newsstand across the street and get me a paper."

I ran back down the steps eager to fulfill the task given to me so we could start with whatever plans he had made for us.

There weren't any.

On returning with the paper, and still with a grin on his face, he said, "Ok, you can go now."

All he wanted was for me to run an errand for him, nothing more. I slowly descended down the stairs and out the door. Walking down the street to rejoin my friends, I could feel tears welling up in my eyes; I was heartbroken. I can remember thinking, "I wonder if my daddy and I will ever do anything together?"

We never did.

I was only nine years old.

I can recall only three other times that I, along with my sister, were summoned up to the apartment. It was when a friend named "Ray" came to visit. Dad would call down to mom-mom's house and tell us with much enthusiasm and excitement , "Ray's here!" "C'mon up as quick as you can; he wants to see you!"

We would hurriedly tidy up ourselves to look present-able, and then run together up the street to the apartment. These were the *only times* our "father" ever asked to see us.

Our relationship with our new "mother", our step-mother Agnes, and her daughter Joan, got off to a slow start. Joan was five years older than Judy and I, and that in itself was not helpful in bringing about a close relationship. We rarely saw each other, the usual exceptions being on holidays, birthdays, or our annual vacation trip to Crystal Beach.

And obviously our social circles were greatly different, given the difference in our ages. She was very popular throughout her school years, and she would eventually become the head majorette at Prospect Park High School, leading the school band at the half-time performances during football season.

So, there it was; for the majority of our formative years Judy and I had no real adult figures in which to bond with. We grew up supporting each other, a blessing that I am grateful for even to this day. In the area of physical needs were never in want, that was never a problem. Emotionally, however, we just wondered if we ever belonged.

Again, there was no structure to our lives during these early years, and in a way we could have been lightly referred to as "street munchkins", left on our own, day after day until dusk. That would change drastically though, after "dad" built his house. Until then, as Judy would say, "We were on our own clock."

Judy seemed to bond quickly with Agnes and Joan after the move to Madison Avenue and our new home. It was almost a necessity, as all three of them took a real disliking to "Bill." Me? I needed a male figure in which I could bond with, but there wasn't any. Even at that young age it became obvious to me my "father" and I would never be close. There just was never any interest on his part.

We all got along pretty well, even though I must admit I was the most difficult of all to associate with. I always regarded myself as a "fifth wheel" in the family, and I was angry and resentful for it. My belief, then and now, was those feelings were justified, and I will be dealing with "the reasons why" as my story unfolds.

Judy and I had a lot of adjustments to make after the move. We went from being "on our own clock" to a very rigid and structured home life. There were many, many

rules and dad made them all; Agnes had no say in anything. He "ruled the roost" with an iron hand, and many times he would change the rules on a whim. He could be very unreasonable at any time, and *that* is one description of him we would all agree on.

He was every bit the household dictator, everything would be done his way. No opinion or input from anyone else in the family, including his wife, mattered. Even his mother, who was not in the habit of criticizing her son, would say of him, "Bill can be a little selfish"; an understatement to be sure.

Judy's pet name for him would eventually be "the warden", and I referred to him as "the Baron", much to the amusement of Agnes and Joan. Of course, we were very careful not to use those terms within his hearing.

Unfortunately Judy and I were never able to get close to our stepmother. She was primarily focused on her daughter Joan, which is reasonable, but she never expressed a desire to build a relationship with either of the two of us. At no time did she ever show any level of affection towards us; not that she disliked us, I just think she regarded us as "baggage" that came along with the marriage.

The Lord is close to the brokenhearted and saves those who are crushed in spirit.

—Psalm 34:18 (NIV)

CHAPTER FOUR

SCARS

NOT ALL BAD

Scars!
Scars are physical evidence of injury, pain, and healing. And they usually remind us of the incident or occasion when we received them, whether by accident or surgery.

Mom-mom and Pop-pop's backyard was half grass and half garden. The garden was used for her great passion for growing flowers; and only one specific kind, Giant Dahlias.

Sometime during every Winter she would pore over her gardening catalogs to determine her selection of bulbs to order for the Spring planting. I don't recall exactly when she had started her hobby but it must have been before we moved in with her. By the time we were teenagers she had a garden of 60 to 80 plants, and her avocation was not a cheap undertaking. I know that in the 50's these unusually large bulbs were priced between ten and fifteen dollars apiece, which was a hefty amount for the times. With that in mind she usually limited herself to ordering only six bulbs per year.

There was a considerable amount of work to be done in order to maintain this endeavor. The bulbs that had been planted in the Spring were dug up in the Fall, placed in bushel baskets and stored in the basement to protect them from Winter's frost. This of course meant they had to be replanted again the next Spring, and this cycle was repeated every year. These plants would grow in excess of four feet and it was necessary to stake them for support. And the task of providing the stakes was given to Judy and me, after a fashion.

Our job was to collect the discarded Christmas trees when the holiday season was over. This was long before artificial trees were available and either families had a live tree or they did not have one.

We would go up and down the street on trash day and drag these trees back home to the backyard. There Pop-pop would have a tremendous bonfire, burning off the branches and leaving only the charred stubble and trunk. At no time can I recall any of the neighbors being alarmed or objecting to this practice. It was not at all unusual in those days to burn combustible waste in one's own backyard. It was a very common chore, especially in the Fall when it seemed that everyone was burning leaves. In time, however, Borough ordinances would curtail all such practices. In the meantime the preparation of the stakes was a yearly event as many of the poles had to be replaced due to weathering and decay.

So Pop-pop would tend the fire with his ever present trusty cigar clenched tightly between his teeth, and with a garden rake in one hand and the garden hose in the other. I think it gave him some sense of control but I am not sure that was really the case.

When the fire was completely out, encouraged by the garden hose, Pop-pop would use a hatchet to chop off the stubble leaving only the trunk. Walla! -- stakes for the garden!

No, the neighbors were not bothered by the fires. They were more apt to be offended by the stench of the truckloads of manure that he brought in for fertilizing the garden in the Spring. But this produced a garden of very rich soil, inhabited by a host of earthworms.

One Spring day, Bill McKee, a classmate of mine, and I decided we would go fishing. The neighboring borough, Ridley Park, had a small lake that was popular for young people to try their hand at catching some of the yellow perch that were plentiful there.

Knowing that we would need bait, and knowing that Mom-mom's garden was an excellent source, we commandeered a pitchfork from the shed under the back porch and set to work. "The harvest is plentiful but the laborers are few", a scripture verse addressing an entirely different subject, of course; but for me and Bill it was more like, "The harvest is plentiful and we don't need any other helpers!!" It was not taking us very long to collect the needed enticements for our fishing expedition.

Things were going well, but then something happened.

Bill was wielding the pitchfork and I was collecting the bounty. At one point our timing was off, or together, depending on ones perspective. I had proceeded to pluck some worms from a clump of dirt the same time Bill thrust the garden tool into the ground.

There was a sharp pain, then nothing; but it was apparent that I was in trouble. As Bill lifted the fork my hand came up with it, and Bill and I were horrified at what we saw.

One of the blades had impaled the ring finger of my right hand on it. The force of the blow was such that my finger was now positioned halfway up the blade. It had entered the top of the finger, glanced off the knuckle, chipping it, and exited through the underside of the finger.

Luckily, I resisted the impulse to jerk my hand away. Instead, Bill held the garden tool motionless while I took my left hand and gently slid my finger off the blade.

Surprisingly that procedure did not hurt at all. Instead it produced a weird sensation, a feeling of intense cold. I felt as if my finger, hand, and forearm just had some ice water poured over them. In later years, as a student of military history, I would wonder if that what was meant by the phrase "cold steel", referring to the use of a bayonet during combat.

Only when my hand was free of the pitchfork did the painful throbbing begin, and the bleeding became profuse.

I left a trail of blood through the backyard, up the porch steps, through the kitchen, and up the stairs to the bathroom. At that point I must have been focusing on the pain and the bleeding as I don't clearly recall what happened next. I know that our grandmother was working at her store up the street, but I don't remember how she found out about the accident or when she arrived to attend to my injury.

My next memory was of her going next door to Dr. Melrath, a chiropractor, for help. He came over to the house and filled the bathroom sink with lukewarm water. He then emptied almost half of a box of salt in it, stirred it for a few seconds, and then placed my hand in the sink. WOW! Did that smart! But it was necessary. It was important to thoroughly clean the wound, given the nature of the contents of the garden. I winced as he massaged my finger to wash out the dirt and manure and it seemed to me that it was taking forever. Of course, I bled; and the sink looked like we had just slaughtered a pig or something. At my age I probably thought that I was bleeding to death. I was only ten years old and I was upset and crying. But I was crying because of the salt in the wound and not because of any fear. Of course, Mom-mom with her sense of compassion (read sarcasm here) labeled me a "sissy".

My friend Bill? He was nowhere to be found. As I was running up the back porch steps he was running home. He was also scared, but probably because he thought that he was in some kind of trouble. He wasn't of course; it was an accident, pure and simple, and our friendship did not suffer for it.

The finger healed quickly without any problems with infection or any permanent damage to the knuckle. It was as if the accident had never happened. The small scars left from that experience are hardly noticeable, and the only time that I might be reminded of the injury is if I am in a hardware store and happen to notice one of those dastardly, evil garden tools—a pitchfork! To my own amusement I might think, "Yes! I see you over there, and I know what you did!"

I have other physical scars as well but it is not necessary to relate them here. The episode that I have just shared is sufficient to support the point I wish to make.

Not all scars are physical; some are emotional, and one can be reminded of them as well. We are apt to remember those more readily than the physical ones because they can be brought to our attention by the simplest means. This is particularly true of the abused.

One of mom-moms favorite implements of punishment was the use of wire coat hangers. She would hold Judy or me by the arm with one hand and administer the "discipline" with the other, and always across bare thighs and calves. This would produce welts on our legs that would last for many days. She knew that it was time to quit only when our legs could no longer support us and our knees buckled.

Sufficient to say that in the late 40's there were no agencies that dealt with the issue of child abuse.

Today, it would be easy to be reminded of those times by the simple act of hanging a shirt on a wire hangar. However, I have long ago dealt with those memories and it troubles me no more. Reminded? Sure! The thoughts will return for a moment but I choose to let them pass on by. On the other hand, I am not sure that Judy has come to terms with those memories; to this day no one will find a wire coat hangar *anywhere* in her home.

As for me, the process of healing from the verbal abuse has taken much more time than any abuse inflicted on me physically.

Humiliation was another method of "discipline" that was administered by both Mom-mom and our "dad."

When Judy and I were teenagers there were times for both of us when someone would remark about how nice our teeth were. Oh, there was a reason for that; or at least it probably contributed to it.

If we forgot to brush our teeth when we were small we would have a toothbrush hung around our neck on a string. In addition, we had to wear a sign in the same fashion that read, "I forgot to brush my teeth". We were made to wear them for the entire day, much to the amusement and ridicule of our peers. The humiliation was horrible.

Now, of course, I still brush my teeth; or at least the few that remain that are of the original equipment, and the sight of a toothbrush is but a momentary reminder.

What will really trigger those painful memories is a particular photo of the WWII Italian dictator, Benito Mussolini. Again, because of my interest in military history there are times when I will come across a photo of him addressing his people from a balcony. He is seen positioned with his arms folded, nose in the air, with a facial expression of pompous arrogance, authority, and power.

It often-times reminds me of one particular incident when I was pushed out the front door wearing those "necklaces". As she shoved me out the door, Mom-mom said to me, "If you dare take those off I will beat you to within an inch of your life!" With that she stood there, arms folded with a belt dangling from her right hand, and peered out through the door-length Venetian blinds to make sure that I complied. Luckily for me, it was early in the morning and none of the other kids were yet out and about.

I just went to the curb and sat there.

Every few minutes I would sneak a subtle side glance that would tell me if she was still there watching. When I was absolutely sure that she had left the door, I went around to the side of the house where I could position myself out of sight behind a Japanese maple tree and the exterior part of the fireplace. I stayed there all day.

These are but a few examples of the kinds of treatment that Judy and I were subjected to in our youth. There were others, and when it came to Bill Ling there were issues that both Judy and Joan had that I did not.

Scars!

We all have them, both physical and emotional, and for some people theirs are more intense than for others.

It was a rough childhood, but Judy and I both realize that it could have been much worse. We are well aware that our experiences turn pale when compared to what others have suffered.

Ginger Farrow is the co-founder and former president of Finders Keepers, an adoption research and support group in Bear, Delaware. She claims that statistics show that as much as forty percent of all children adopted suffer some form of abuse. How tragic! And, I take issue with people who have never been habitually exposed to such treatment who might glibly remark, "Forget it, it's in the past". Such people have no real understanding of the long range effects of continual abusive treatment.

There are still some people alive today that need only to drive past a tattoo parlor or examine the numbers permanently etched on their own arms to be reminded of their own personal horrors of abuse. Immediately, it will bring to mind memories of infamous places with names such as Buchenwald and Auschwitz. To tell them to "Forget it" borders on insensitive callousness.

I need to tell you now that when Judy and I discussed the writing of this book she had admonished me not to make it too negative. She said that if I did no one would want to read it. She has a point. Still, it is imperative to show where I have been before I can show people where the Lord has brought me. So, as the radio commentator Paul Harvey might suggest, you need to press on to know "The Rest of the Story".

> Oh Lord, you will keep us safe and protect us from such people forever.
>
> —Psalm 12:7 (NIV)

I have never been one to indulge in character assassination and I don't intend to start now. It is a trait I have observed in some people and something I absolutely detest. Perhaps it is because I have been the recipient of such treatment in the past.

That is not to say that I have never made a disparaging remark about another individual, I have; we all have. But to make a concerted effort to methodically tear down a person's character is simply not a trait of mine.

So, for me to portray Irene B. Tunison, Mom-mom, as a totally mean, hateful, vindictive person; something of a matronly ogre, would be grossly unfair.

There was a side of her that was a truly loving, caring, and giving person. It was not that she didn't possess these traits, the problem was that she was <u>selective</u> to whom she showed them to.

Our adoptive grandmother was the one who essentially raised us and not Bill Ling. There was little, if any, real interaction of a father towards his children by him. Almost all of our physical and material needs were provided by her and Pop-pop. Most of the family believes that it was a price that she was willing to pay to keep "dad" safe from the war.

Judy and I were never in want of anything; that is, nothing <u>material.</u> That is a point I must make perfectly clear. The house we lived in was nothing special but it was comfortable, and certainly on a par with the rest of the dwellings in the neighborhood. We shared a middle bedroom when we were very young. Later, when it was appropriate to separate us, Judy would occupy the front bedroom and I had the back bedroom; vacated by our "father" after he met and married Agnes.

What I remember most about this time was that Mom-mom had huge "bolsters" for our twin beds in the winter-time. They were bed-length pillow-type mattresses filled with goose down. She would fluff them up with her hands while we waited patiently for them to be "ready". Then dad would pick us up, one by one, and on the count of "three!" playfully throw us into bed. We would be totally engulfed by the bolster. The depression made by our bodies created a small wall of pillow all around us. As children we looked forward to this playful bedtime activity and it is one of the *very few* good memories of our childhood.

Where our care from our grandparents really excelled was in the providing of our food and clothing. The very fact that they owned their own market gave us a tremendous advantage in both the variety and freshness of the foodstuffs available to us. Simply put, we ate good; that is, when we finally got around to eating.

Mom-mom was meticulous in providing our clothing. We always had clean, neat clothing to wear. She did the wash every Monday and the ironing on Tuesday. These were very laborious jobs for women in those days. There were no automatic washers or steam irons in the 40's.

She had a double-tub washer, one tub for washing and the other for rinsing. I can still visualize her hand cranking the rollers that would squeeze the soap out of the material and then drop the item into the rinse tub. Wash day was a hard working day and consumed a lot of time. There were no clothes dryers; everything had to hand carried to the backyard and hung on clotheslines for drying. I can still remember helping her take down the clothes from the lines in the wintertime. Often they would be frozen, stiff like cardboard; they would then be hung in the basement to complete the drying.

Ironing was another day-long job. She had a coke bottle filled with water which had a small sprinkler head attached to it. She would then sprinkle some water on the article to be ironed and then iron it with a common electric iron. That was the "steaming" process used in those days. And everything was ironed. Housewives today would probably raise their eyebrows to know that in those days even the bed sheets and pillowcases were ironed!

Mom-mom's second great love was sewing. She had what today would be considered a true antique. It was a treadle powered Singer sewing machine. The sewing mechanism was set into motion by rocking the treadle platform with a heel-toe motion of the feet. A belt would rotate and drive the gears that provided the power needed to do the sewing. She made curtains, bedspreads, and a lot of Judy's and my clothing. She would have several works in progress at the same time, with sewing patterns strewn all over the dining room table. What clothes she didn't make she bought for us, and they were always nice and of good quality.

Christmas and birthdays were a real treat. No token celebrations there! We always had nice gifts and plenty of them; probably more so than most of the kids in the neighborhood. Birthday parties were celebrated with neighborhood friends and classmates, and it was always our grandmother who planned and paid for everything. Our dad was *never involved* in any of it.

It was also true that Mom-mom and Pop-pop had tender hearts towards the needy. At Thanksgiving and Christmas they would use the resources they had at their store to make holiday baskets for the families that lived along Darby Creek. These were very low income families with not much resources of their own, and some of the families bordered on outright poverty.

Our grandparents would have both the dining room and kitchen tables cluttered with the best food choices that money could buy. And for the children there was always an array of candies and fruit included. Whatever those families were going to have or not have during the holidays, one thing was certain, they were going to have a good meal!

Also, when I worked in their store as a teenager there were times when a homeless person would come in and, visibly embarrassed, ask if they could have a sandwich. Without exception, not only would Mom-mom or Pop-pop make the sandwich with the best of luncheon meats and cheeses, they would literally pack him a lunch. I never remember it being less than a sandwich, fruit, a candy bar, and a soft drink or milk.

Pop-pop explained to me that the Great Depression years were still fresh in their minds; a time when people fell on "hard times" through no fault of their own. He would say, "Your life can fall apart very quickly, without any warning". Little did I know at the time that I would be experiencing that very thing in years to come.

So, there was never any question of our physical needs being met; that was never an issue. The problem lay in our emotional needs; the need of a sense of safety, love, acceptance, and belonging. Especially in the area of self-esteem; I would be the recipient of very harsh treatment, which I will deal with later in this book.

Aunt Bernice would tell us many years later that indeed there were two sides to Mom-mom. Either because of a flaw in her personality, or by her own design, she would purposely favor one person over another in *any* family. It was very obvious that she favored Kenny over Joan, and Judy over me. And whenever our cousins Kenny and Joan were around Judy would make the remark, "We don't even exist". She wasn't wrong.

Our aunt said that she, Mom-mom, would even do this with her own children! Bill Ling could never do anything wrong, and Aunt Bernice could do nothing right. To emphasize the fact that she understood our dilemma, she shared with us one particular example from her own childhood.

She said that when she and Bill were teenagers, Bill had asked for a radio for his birthday. When his birthday came he got one. Then when Aunt Bernice's birthday approached she also asked for a radio. Her birthday gift was a pair of socks; and her mother's explanation to her was, "You'll take what you get and like it!"

Such was Irene B. Tunison; a strange person, a chameleon, a type of Jekyll and Hyde. But she was "not all bad", and to imply that she was, is simply just not fair.

I will be glad and rejoice in your love, for you saw my affliction and knew the anguish of my soul.
—Psalm 31:7 (NIV)

CHAPTER FIVE

TRAGEDY

SIGNS

One of the chores in my youth that was my responsibility was to make sure the lawns were cut.

Lawns, plural!

Initially there were two, the lawn at our grandparents house, and the backyard to the apartments over the store and Laundromat. Eventually there would be a third, and on occasion, a fourth.

The third lawn would be the one on Madison Avenue when dad built our home there in 1954. The fourth was the one to the cottage our grandparents owned at Crystal Beach Manor, Maryland. That chore was not an ongoing one, as the cottage was rented out weekly for most of the summer. Usually it was my job in the early spring, when the property was being prepared for those rentals, and again during our two weeks vacation there in August.

It was a laborious job. Mostly because the work was performed using the old push-type reel mowers. Power mowers were not readily available until 1954. I remember the year because, once again, it was when we moved from Mom-mom's house to our new home.

One summer afternoon I was in the process of cutting the front lawn of dad's house just as he was returning home from work. Our neighbor was out in his own yard and yelled over to dad, "When are you going to get a power mower?" Dad's reply was, "I already have one", and pointed to me. All three of us had a good laugh! It was a joke, and a good one, and I took it as such.

The 'power' required to operate these push mowers were strong shoulders and arms; and the golden-rule was to keep the lawns cut short. Also, one hoped that there would not be any extended periods of rain. Tall grass or wet grass, the two detriments to making any progress using these particular types of mowers. Either situation would find you 'stalled' after cutting only about a four foot swath. The cutting mechanism was just not efficient enough to handle the volume in front of the mower if the grass was tall. That, or wet grass, would seize up the mower, and one had no other option than to stop and clean out the debris binding the reel and the cutting blade.

It was not unusual for some of the lawn to grow faster, and taller, in some areas than others; especially when the grass was close to the houses or fences. This entailed using a hand sickle to chop down the grass to a height where the use of the mower could be employed; and what we would now consider to be a simple job, could back then be a very difficult and time consuming one.

This was particularly true after vacationing at the beach in August. I returned to three lawns that had two weeks of growth to them and it always involved the use of a sickle before cutting. It was very hard work. Vacation was always fun, but I dreaded what was facing me when I got back home.

One particular Friday, before our move to Madison Avenue, I had finished cutting the lawn to the apartments and the front lawn at Mom-mom's house. I was tired. My back was aching from all the bending over while engaging the use of the sickle on the lawns and then, of course, cutting them. I asked my grandmother if I could let the backyard left undone until Saturday morning. Mom-mom gave her permission with the stipulation that I was not to do anything else until the chore was finished. Of course, I agreed.

Early Saturday morning I was in the process of completing this particular chore when I heard, "Yo, Gene!", from around the side of the house. This was the typical beckoning call my friends and I used to summon each other in the early mornings. It was Pat Fries. I had forgotten that earlier in the week we had made plans to ride our bikes over to the "five and ten" on Lincoln Avenue, six blocks away. Pat asked me, "Are you still going?" "Yeah, I replied, but Mom-mom said I have to finish the lawn first, but it won't take too long." "Okay", he responded, "Why don't Billy and I meet you over there?" "Billy?" I inquired; "Is he going too?" "Yeah, he wants to go with us, OK?" "Sure", I said, "I should be done in another fifteen minutes, or so; sure you don't want to wait?" "Nah", said Pat, We'll just meet you over there." "Okay", I replied, "See you in a couple minutes." And with that, off they went on their way, and I returned to my work.

There is a phrase that says, "The early bird gets the worm"; for the Fries children it was, "The early bird gets the bike". There was only one bike in their family, for the four of them old enough to ride, and the one who was up and out first in the morning was the one who got it. For that reason the boys were apt to sneakily ride double, a practice that Mrs. Fries had established a rule against. It was obvious that on this day Pat was going to "sidestep" that rule and allow his younger brother on the bike with him. The year was 1951; I was eleven, Pat was ten years of age, and Billy, six.

When I was finished cutting the grass, I hurriedly put the mower under the back porch and traded it for my bike; and off I went to catch up with Pat and Billy.

I pedaled hard up Summit Avenue to the crest, and then sat back down on the seat and leisurely pedaled the remaining hundred yards or so to the intersection at 9th Avenue. Then a left turn on "9th" and an easy glide down the hill to Pennsylvania Avenue, approximately another thirty yards. Turning right onto "Pennsylvania", I could see Pat and Billy approaching me on their return trip from the store. We passed each other. As I continued on, steering over close to the right-hand curb to initiate a "U" turn; I heard the sounds that have never left me.

A horn, a high pitched squeal of hard pressed brakes, a crash, screams, and then for a moment—silence.

I had been spared the sight of the actual impact, but not its aftermath. Pat and Billy had rode their bike into the path of a large beer-distributor truck coming down the hill, the same hill I had come down on 9th Avenue. The two men who had been in the truck were now racing back to Patrick lying tangled in the twisted mess that was once his bicycle. One of the men diverted his direction to the nearest house to summon an ambulance. The other man was "beside himself" with grief and anguish, crying profusely, and saying over and over, "Oh, No!" "God, Please, No!"

Billy lay motionless, and lifeless, against the curb; blood all over it, across the grassy median and onto the sidewalk. It is a sight that I have never forgotten.

I was traumatized by what I saw, unable to move or utter a word. I was horrified and shaking; and it wasn't until one of the men asked me, "Do you know these kids?", that

I was able to interrupt the thoughts racing through my mind as to what I had just witnessed. I answered with a weak "Yeah, They're my friends from across the street." He yelled, "Go get their mother!" I was overwhelmed with fear so much that I couldn't respond verbally. I just shook my head and started off for Mrs. Fries' house. I was shaking so uncontrollably that I could not bring myself to climb up on my bike. I raced up the hill as fast as I could, pushing the two-wheeler alongside me. It would be a good two months before I could again attempt to ride it.

I can remember arriving at Mrs. Fries' house and pushing the bike on its way into their front yard, letting it crash alone onto the ground. I raced to the house and repeatedly rang the bell and banged on the door. Almost immediately Pat and Billy's mother answered the door and she knew that something was terribly wrong. "Gene!" she said. "What's wrong?!" "Mrs. Fries!" I replied, sobbing, "Pat and Billy just got hit by a truck up on 9th Avenue!" Not a very tactful way to break terrible news, but then, I was only eleven years old. The second thing I can vividly remember about this tragedy is the look of stark, overwhelming fear on her face when I told her. Even after all this time I can still visualize that look in my minds eye.

She rushed past me down the front steps, not bothering to shut any doors. She then ran up in the middle of the street to 9th Avenue and the accident scene. As she did so, I could hear her praying, her voice fading from my hearing as she put distance between us; "Hail Mary, Full of Grace; the Lord is with thee….."

I was running up Summit Avenue in the opposite direction to Tunison's Market to tell Mom-mom what had just happened. I was crying.

Pat would be totally unaware of all that had transpired following the very moment of impact. He would not regain consciousness until after arriving at the hospital; and I can never remember hearing about his response to the news of his brothers death. It was just something that I and his other friends never brought up; surmising he was having a difficult enough time dealing with that tragedy on his own, without any of us reminding him of that fateful day.

In the months that followed I would replay, relive, that event over and over in my mind. I was trying to make some sense out of it, but I could not. Then the "what if?" thoughts started to plague me.

"What if", Pat and Billy had waited for me to finish my chore? We would have been well past the intersection at 9th and Pennsylvania Avenues when the truck came down that hill, and the accident would have never happened. "What if", Billy had not gone with Pat? The accident may still have happened but Billy would still be alive. And finally, "what if" I had cut the backyard the day before, Friday, and my chores had been completed. Would I have also been involved in the accident itself?

Thoughts like these are easy to contemplate, and tempt one to fantasize about being able to "rewrite" the events and cause a change. But we are not in that position to do so.

It is God who is in control, and as hard as it may be at times, we have to recognize His sovereignty and believe that He has a purpose for everything that happens. We often cannot make any sense out of such tragedies, but then, I do not think that we are supposed to.

He tells us in the book of Isaiah, which supports my belief, and says; "For my thoughts are not your thoughts, neither are your ways my ways," declares the Lord. "As the heavens are higher than the earth so are my ways higher than your ways and my thoughts than your thoughts." (Isaiah 55: 8, 9 NIV)

Today, as a Christian, these words from the Lord are what I cling to when things happen that are beyond my control and understanding.

The result of the experience of the accident caused me to have many nightmares. Not the waking-up-screaming type, but I would oftentimes wake myself crying.

I cried a lot.

Judy can remember the two of us sitting on the front steps to our grandparent's house, both weeping, watching the many people go to the Fries' house for the viewing. It was commonplace in those days for a funeral to be conducted in the home where the deceased had lived.

I would intermittently break out in sobbing for many days to come; I just could not get those images of the accident out of my mind. One day Mom-mom, irritated, said to me, "Quit your damn crying, you big baby!" Of course, that was easy for her to say; she had not been there; she did not witness firsthand the carnage that I had.

Then came the "clincher", a comment that would instill the fear of God in me, an unhealthy one, for many years to come. Referring to the accident, she said, "See, that's what God does to children who don't obey their parents!"

I took it to heart. Why shouldn't I? After all, at my young age children look to their parents for knowledge and direction. They have wisdom; they know about life, they know about "things." It was because of that comment that I envisioned God to be a "celestial bully", almost sadistic, ready to pounce on me whenever I got out of line. It instilled in me the erroneous belief that my standing with him was a function of "works", of performance, and how good a person I was.

Even at that early age I could see how seemingly impossible it was to measure up, and doubted if anyone could really know if they were going to heaven or hell. It also ingrained in me a morbid preoccupation on the subject of death. I felt like my life could be snuffed out at any moment and I was afraid of dying; and whatever waited for me afterwards. Surprising thoughts for a boy so young, however, if someone where to ask me when it was I thought the Lord had started working in my spirit; started "sowing seeds", I would say it was during this early part of my life. For, as part of the lyrics to the classic hymn "Amazing Grace" goes; "Twas grace that taught my heart to _fear_....."

> The fear of the Lord is the beginning of knowledge; but fools despise wisdom and discipline.
> —Proverbs 1:7 (NIV)

The road that was the entrance to Crystal Beach had an archway with two large white pillars on either side of the road and a large arching sign overtop which read, "Crystal Beach Manor." It was all but considered a local landmark. So much so, that there was a tavern on the approach-way that coined the name for their business as the "Archway Inn." This business enterprise had no affiliation with the beach property itself.

The summer rentals at our grandparents cottage did not start until June 1st, and periodically there would be day trips to the beach so our grandparents could accomplish some of the tasks to be done in preparation for those rentals. Since their business demanded most of their attention, Mom-mom and Pop-pop would "make a day of it", trying to finish as much work as possible while there. Mrs. Fries, now a trusted and knowledgeable employee, would oversee the running of the store business in our grandparents absence.

The cottage had been closed up for the entire Fall and Winter and now needed a complete cleaning. That under-taking was essentially entirely Mom-mom's responsibility. Pop-pop would normally be with us for only one of these excursions. He could usually finish up "the man's work" in one day. This entailed taking down the heavy storm windows and replacing them with the summer screens; no air conditioning during those times! I can still picture him setting up those wooden saw horses and placing some of the frames on them to be re-screened. Often there was some minor painting to be done, and of course, the pump to the well had to be checked and, at times, maintenance performed.

As usual, during these annual events our cousins Kenny and Joan would join us. The four of us being very close during those early years; it would not be until we were much more mature before Judy and I would notice that Mom-mom's attention favored our cousins over us. And, after all that had transpired through the years we suspect that it may have been because they were "blood" and we were not. Later on, we would drift apart, but at this stage in our lives we looked forward to this time together.

One time our grandmother inadvertently started something that would become a ritual whenever the four of us were together for this trip. As we approached the archway to the beach she started singing a little repetitive jingle, "I see the sign, I see the sign." We all picked up on it and after awhile it became a contest and a hallmark of the excursion. Whoever saw the sign first would start the jingle, and after a few moments Mom-mom would have a quartet riding in the car with her. It was one of those little, simple, nonsensical things that everyone seems to remember about their childhood.

Signs!

They are everywhere!

They give us information, direction, and sometimes warning: "Philadelphia, 13 Miles"; "Hospital, Left at light"; "Caution, Falling Rock." And; who of us has not, at some time or another, have been relieved (no pun intended) to see that all important sign that simply says, "Restrooms?"

Sometime when I was twelve years old I started a paper route. I had dealt with the traumatic results of the accident, to a degree, and was now again riding my bike.

The garage where we would go to pick up our papers was located at the intersection of Chester Pike and Lincoln Avenue, which were the two main thoroughfares through Prospect Park. I would ride up Summit Avenue, turn right onto Chester Pike and past "our" store on the corner; then coast down the long hill to the intersection and garage.

On Sunday mornings I was off to do my deliveries early, since I had to be back home in time to get ready for Sunday school. I would usually start out about 6 am, and there was absolutely NO traffic on the streets. I would ride my bike down the middle of Chester Pike with no cars in sight in either direction. I was even surprised at myself that I would do this, given the experience that I had just the year before. I repeatedly checked for traffic coming from behind me but there never was any. I can remember the first few times that I did this. It seemed strange, you were looking at everything that was familiar to you at a different angle, a different perspective, and in some ways it seemed as if you were seeing it for the first time.

During this trip there was a sign that I knew that I was not seeing for the first time. It was a sign that no one could miss, and very familiar to the residents of the town.

At the bottom of Chester Pike there was an appliance store on the left-hand side with a huge neon sign erected on the roof. The letters had to be at least six feet tall and must have cost the owner of the store a small fortune to have made. It could been seen from great distances at night with its bright, red lettering beaming its message. There were only two words, all in capital lettering; "JESUS SAVES."

Even though I was aware of the sign being there in the past, I had given no thought to its meaning. But now it was in my view every day on my way to pick up my papers. It started to haunt me. "What does it mean?" I thought; "What is it trying to tell me?" "JESUS SAVES", "saves what?"

I tried ignoring those thoughts but it was not working; they just would not leave me alone.

I could not figure it out and I was too afraid to ask; especially not anyone at home. Almost anything I would ask about was considered to be "a dumb question", and I knew that I risked criticism and ridicule so I just let it pass. I could have asked my Sunday school teacher but I was too shy to do so. I was not in the habit of doing anything that would bring attention to myself. Anyhow, I knew that I had already sealed my fate.

I had never "played hooky" from public school, but I did from Sunday school. I was made to attend, and at times when I did not want to go I was labeled a "heathen". It was a statement I would find strange coming from a woman who *never* attended church. The only time I can remember Irene B. Ling Tunison being in a church was at my wedding.

On this particular Sunday I headed for my Sunday school class at the Olivet Presbyterian Church at 10th and Washington streets, approximately seven blocks away. But instead of continuing to what was supposed to be my destination, I changed directions and circled around the block and walked to the Norwood Diner.

I spent my Sunday school hour there, and the collection money, before returning home. "Now I've done it!" I thought . "That's it! I'm done for; I'm going to hell for sure!" I had just spent the collection money, a quarter, God's money, on a donut and a Coke!

Signs; yes, they are everywhere. And, when I reflect on that sign which was a Prospect Park landmark, a sign that is no longer there, I now know and understand its message.

"JESUS SAVES", was a sign that could be said put forth all three categories that I have previously mentioned; information, direction, and warning.

Its information from God the Father is, "For God so loved the world that he gave his one and only Son, that whoever believes in him shall not perish but have eternal life." (John 3:16 NIV)

The <u>direction</u> is from Jesus, the Son; "…. I am the way and the truth and the life. No one comes to the Father except through me." (John 14:6 NIV)

And, from The Holy Spirit, a stern <u>warning</u>; "But since you rejected me when I called and no one gave heed when I stretched out my hand, since you ignored all my advice and would not accept my rebuke, I in turn will laugh at your disaster; I will mock when calamity overtakes you- when calamity over takes you like a storm, when disaster sweeps over you like a whirlwind, when distress and trouble overwhelm you. Then they will call to me but I will not answer; they will look for me but will not find me. Since they hated knowledge and did not choose to fear the Lord" (Proverbs 1:24-29 NIV) Yes, Jesus Saves!—a powerful message! "JESUS SAVES"— for me, a powerful sign!

> He sends from heaven and saves me, rebuking those who hotly pursue me; God sends his love and his faithfulness.
>
> —Psalm 57:3 (NIV)

CHAPTER SIX

CARD GAMES

ACCEPTANCE

The legal age for a young adult during the decade that was the "50's" was twenty- one, and not eighteen as it is today. Back then, during that era, an eighteen-year-old could not vote, sign a binding contract of any kind, or even rent an apartment; the possible exception being those away at college, and most probably their parents signed the lease.

It is necessary to establish this fact before continuing this portion of my story and the reason for it will become evident at its conclusion.

One of the most important of all emotional needs a human-being has is the need of acceptance. To an individual it conveys worth, importance, and belonging. Rejection has an opposite effect. It signals the person is of little importance, not valued; that he or she does not "fit in".

Without seeming like I am indulging in a "pity party", or "sour grapes", I can *objectively* put myself in the second category during the course of my childhood. Rejection, experienced within the family, was the norm for me, primarily initiated by our grandmother, and more subtly by dad.

Any question I would ask was considered by Mom-mom to be a "dumb question", any comment or opinion by me on *any* subject was deemed a "stupid comment". This was particularly true when the four of us children were together, cousins Kenny and Joan, and my sister and me. Any time I would attempt to join in a conversation our grandmother would shut me down with remarks such as; "What would you know about it?, You don't know anything, ya dummy!" or, "Who asked you?, Nobody asked you, stay out of it!."

Invariably it would precipitate a round of laughter from the other three, as they would think it to be funny. For me, it resulted in a feeling of hurt, humiliation and rejection. Judy would later call it "kids stuff", but then, she was not the one continually on the receiving end of it all. It would seem that I was at the end of the "pecking order", and as hard as I might try to have equal standing with Mom-mom, as the other three had, it was not ever going to happen. It was the niche that was chiseled out for me and it never did change. Of course, at this young age, from about eight years old and onward, I did not have the astuteness to figure out what was going on, but there would be an incident at the family's Christmas dinner table when I was fourteen years old that would open my eyes as to what was really happening.

These were not isolated incidents or occasional sporadic episodes; it was a steady diet of emotional abuse and rejection. I began to withdrawal from being involved, slipping into becom- ing a solitary person. At first this was not a conscious decision on my part, but later on it would become a deliberate response to such treatment. But in the meantime, even "being quiet" did not work. When I shied away from participating in their conversations, I was labeled "a bump on a log"; unsociable. Her typical harassing comment would be something like, "Well, don't just sit there like a bump on a log, say something, dummy!"

More laughter, but not mine.

I was in a no-win situation and unable to do anything about it. Any complaint on my part would be considered "sassing", and invariably a sharp slap across the face would follow. Even that would net a chuckle from the other three. It was as if they were giving their stamp of approval to my position in the family.

My one 'saving grace' was that she was consumed with the myriad responsibilities of running the store business. Because of this, we were not in each others company very frequently; and it was my only reprieve.

Judy and I started working at 'Tunison's Market" almost immediately after our grandparents had bought the business in 1948; we were just eight years old. In these early years we did little jobs like marking items and stocking shelves. I was trying to remember when we got our Social Security cards and had emailed Judy to establish whether it was in 1953 or 1954. In my memory I had it placed as 1953 but I was not sure, but her email response to my query indicated that I probably had it correct. Here is her email, verbatim; I think that you will find it both interesting and comical. "

Hi Bro:

We started working for our pocket money at the age of 8 (1948), cutting up boxes from the weekly order and sorting soda bottles in the basement of the store; stocking shelves and marking merchandise. I think we started wait- ing on customers at age 11 and actually sliced lunchmeat at 12. I remember these things because when we cut boxes, I cut my leg badly (still have the <u>scar</u>) with a box cutter. I remember dipping ice-cream that was as hard as a rock, and Tastykakes that melted in the morning sun because Mom-mom had them on a shelf in the front window. I remember we waited on customers long before we were 13 because a lady asked me for Kotex and I pretended I didn't know what that was because Mom-mom hadn't told me about the birds and bees yet. I KNOW that was before I was 13. We bagged 5 lbs of potatoes in bags when we weren't busy,

checked the penny candy shelf, filled up the cigarette slots, etc. When we applied for our social security numbers is a puzzle. But according to my social security statements, Pop-pop reported deductions for me in 1953, on. And remember, you and I , sitting on the floor in the living room, sorting hundreds of invoices and putting them in alphabetical order and then by date....what fun!!! Pop-pop would go to Dock Street early on Friday a.m. to get the produce for the store, Mom-mom would get up early and make salads to be sold. How many cold, cold mornings did you and I have to get ourselves up and fed and out to school on time and never see an adult at home until dinnertime??? Have to go now but can continue on and on and on and on whenever you want..... Love ya, Judy"

My response:

Hi Sis,

Memories!........Yes, I remember the filing, with the stacks of invoices from the vendors almost completely covering the living room rug. It was difficult to move around without stepping on some of the piles. Then when we were finished, we would break out the Canasta cards and play.

I can remember hooking up the garden hose to the close-line and running through the water spray..."camping out" in the pup-tent in the back-yard until the mosquitoes drove us back in the house; sneaking up into the attic to take a peek at the Christmas decorations and the Halloween costumes.......Playing "kick the can" and "Simon says" with all the kids on the street........playing "baseball" in the street and having to run down the ball before it went into the sewer, and if it did we would have to take off the grate and climb down to get it.

I thought about your comments on the 'Kotex' and the remembrance brought back a few things that made me smile. Before we took the cut-up boxes from the store to Chester to sell for scrap, I would have to take them down the street to Mom-mom's backyard. If you remember, Pop-pop had built a large cinder-block fireplace just inside the back gate where we would burn that trash. I would fill up the largest box I could find with that scrap cardboard, and naturally it was the 'Kotex' box. I was still very young then and wasn't strong enough to carry the boxes, I used my wagon. I would tow the box of 'Kotex' and its contents down to the house; and on occasion I would notice some smiles and snickers from the adults on the street. I would wonder, "Why are they laughing?", "I didn't do anything funny!" When I got a little older and knew what they were, I made sure I used the boxes that the cigarettes came in to transport the trash. They were big enough boxes, but yet smaller than the 'Kotex' boxes. Still, I didn't care how many trips it took me to get the trash down to the backyard, I was *never again* going to use "those" boxes!

Another comical event! The order had come in from Quaker Distributors and Pop-pop told me to unpack "this box" (the Kotex box) and put them in paper bags and put them on the shelf next to the cellar-way to the store basement. I remember asking, "What are these things?" (Innocence!) Pop-pop was flustered for a moment, very noticeable, and then just replied, "They're NAPKINS." I thought it strange to be putting napkins in brown paper bags, but before I could ask about it Pop-pop had made his hasty exit!!! Funny!!

Gotta go, Sis, but again, what you have offered is exactly what I am looking for. We both remember different things, and what we do remember will add substantially to the book... Keep it coming!

I'll be glad to see you Saturday...and lunch is on me, I insist! Hugs, Bro Gene.

Ah, yes, Canasta! We played it incessantly!

Friends of ours from up the street, Patsy and Charlie Lowe, had taught Judy how to play and Judy in turn taught me. We were practically addicted to the game, playing hour after hour; day after day; sitting on the living room floor at Mom-mom's house. We just about wore out the double-deck of cards used to play the game, and I think that it was the last great portion of time we spent together. We were twelve years old at this time and we started to slowly drift apart. Mainly because we would develop a different circle of friends, and partly due to the continuing wedge driven between us orchestrated by Mom-mom. We were a little older now, and we were beginning to understand what was going on with our grandmother's unequal treatment towards the two of us. Naturally, I resented it. And even though Judy could recognize what was going on, and dislike it, she was not in any position to do anything about it. There were a few times that she made a token effort to speak out on my behalf but to no avail. She had to be extremely careful in doing this; she clearly understood where the limit was in "dealing" with Mom-mom, and *that* wasn't far! Understandably, Judy wasn't going to over do it and jeopardize her position; for once a person had crossed the line with Irene B. Tunison they were "done." Even she, Mom-mom, was known to repeatedly say, "Once a person crosses me, they're finished!" A forgiving person, our grandmother was not!

Judy and I would eventually both believe that we didn't like each other. It was a most unfortunate development; something that we could never find ourselves to discuss and sort out. This rift between us has lasted for decades, and has just in recent years been resolved in a magnificent way! Without question, the events that have led to the writing of this book has brought us tremendously close, closer than we have ever been before.

I digress! Back to the card game, or rather, games.

Canasta was not the only card game we played during our young years. We had also indulged in the childhood games of "Old Maids," "War," "Go Fish", and of course, "Blackjack."

The game Pinochle never interested me; although Agnes, Judy, and my other sister, Joan, would often prod me to learn. They needed a "fourth" in order to properly play the game, and oftentimes when our Aunt Anna was present, Agnes's sister, out would come the cards and a game would ensue. But for me, I just couldn't be bothered with it.

The only 'game' of Poker that I ever played was one of my own version, a fantasy game in every sense of the word, played by me at the Christmas dinner table in 1954.

The legitimate game was never an avocation of mine, and it was probably good that it was not. I can recall the many times my Air Force buddies in future years would gamble away their service pay playing Poker. They would no sooner get paid that they would cover one of the tables in the 'day room' with one of our blue Air Force blankets, break out the poker chips and start to play. Many of the guys would lose their money in less than an hour, and then seek someone to borrow from until the next payday. I never understood this, given the fact that our service stipend was menial to begin with.

Tunisons' Market was open 364 days a year. The only day it was closed was on Christmas Day. The Christmas dinner was always celebrated at Mom-mom and Pop-pop's house, and she provided the entire meal, a real feast! She would start preparing the meal on Christmas Eve and her work would continue early the next morning, up until the time the dinner was ready to be served. A tremendous amount of work, but we all knew that she liked to cook, and she thoroughly enjoyed putting this celebration meal together. This woman of German heritage knew how to cook. If one could not find something at her table to tickle their taste buds, they were just too darn picky!

I enjoyed these dinners in the very early years, however the time would come when I would absolutely dread them. That was because invariably Mom-mom would use this occasion to openly embarrass and humiliate me in front of the entire family. There was a time when I could expect to be set upon by her sometime during the course of this annual event; and I can vaguely remember these episodes started at about age 10, and were repeated *every* year, without exception; up until the time I left for the Air Force upon graduating from high school.

But in the very early years I looked forward to them. Probably because I looked forward to seeing grand-mom Beeson, Mom-mom's mother, who would always fascinate me with her childhood stories. She was well into her 80's and in a nursing home, but "sharp as a tack" in her mind. I know that she thoroughly enjoyed being with the family, and it was very obvious she took a liking to Judy and me. Perhaps that's why I was always glad to see her, she liked me and I knew it. Her, and my Aunt Bernice; my two childhood champions!

Being as young as I was, 8 and 9 years old, I was in the "cowboy and Indian" stage. Because of this, I would be fined tuned whenever she talked about "The Old West", a part of our culture that I still find somewhat fascinating, truly unique to our American history. I can remember her telling me, "What a time 'we' had with that Apache fellow, Geronimo!"

She always had some great stories to tell and I was always ready to listen.

She had passed away by the time 1954 came along, and the Christmas dinner table now seated the usual family members that were there yearly; and the seating arrangements were almost always the same.

Seated next to me on my right was Joan, our cousin, next to her was her brother Kenny. Then there were their parents, our Uncle Bert and our Aunt Bernice. Continuing around to the right would be Nancy, the late arrival to the Waltson family, now only about five years old; seated next to her mother so that Aunt Bernice could attend to her needs. Next came Pop-pop, then Mom-mom, and seated next to her of course was "dad." Agnes and her daughter, our step-sister Joan, followed. Judy completed the "circle", seated on my left. An even dozen people made up the core of the family.

Sometime well into the dinner Kenny asked for the gravy boat to be passed to him for his potatoes. After using it, he started to put it back down on the table and some of the gravy had run down the outside of the spout and dripped onto Mom-mom's fine linen tablecloth. "Oops! Sorry, Mom-mom" was his apology. Mom-mom prized her fine linen, but her response to this mishap was, " Oh, Don't worry about it, dear. It will come out in the wash." (I remember this verbatim)

A few minutes had elapsed when I asked for the biscuits to be passed to me. In taking one off the plate, the biscuit slipped out of my hand and, "plop!", right into my water glass.

The law of displacement dictates that the water, now occupied by the biscuit in the glass, had to go somewhere. It did. The water overflowed onto the tablecloth. Mom-mom's response to this was, "Butterfingers!, I swear, you can't hold on to anything!"

Again, there was laughter, and again; it wasn't mine.

I just looked at her, which brought the warning, "Don't you give me that look, or I'll come over there and smack it off your face!" More laughter.

Aunt Bernice exclaimed, "Mommmm!" She seemed to understand what was going on and somehow I had the idea that she had experienced, at sometime in her past, similar treatment. She then looked at me and just shook her head. And to this day I can recall what looked like her eyes tearing up with empathy towards me; perhaps reminding herself of painful memories of her own.

Bill Ling said nothing, and, of course, he wouldn't. He, as usual, was the disinterested party; and there was just no way that he was going to challenge anything his mother did. It was as if he gave his official permission for such treatment. Not once can I ever remember him coming to my defense for anything.

I diverted my attention to my plate, toying with my food, and tried not to let my anger and frustration overwhelm me. I refused to cry in response to the humiliation.

My eyes kept wandering back and forth to the two spots on the tablecloth. Gravy and water, water and gravy. I started having a long conversation with myself, an extensive evaluation of all that had just transpired.

"What's going on here", I asked myself. Then I reasoned in my own thinking, "The water will dry out, the gravy might leave a stain." I thought, "Was my accident any worse than Kenny's?" It was then that I realized that it wasn't as much as the mistake that had been made, it only mattered *Who* made it!

I can distinctly remember thinking to myself, "Darn, being in this family is like being in a crap shoot, you never know what's going to happen!" A brief mental pause and then I corrected myself. "No", I thought, "there's too much left to chance in a crap game, and there's no chance involved here; it's more like a poker game!"

I started to fantasize.

"Yeah, a poker game, and there's a dealer in a poker game; one who oversees the flow of the game and deals the cards to the players.", talking to myself in my head.

"That would be Mom-mom", I mused. And I had it tagged right.

She controlled "the game" alright; this great matriarch of the family was "Queen of the Realm." In my mind she was the perpetual dealer, and the deck was stacked. The 'cards dealt' by her represented each persons position in the family, their level of participation, and not everyone was given the same number of cards. I fantasized that we all had been dealt a different number of cards which was anywhere from five down to two. These 'hands' denoted which level each member of the family was <u>permitted</u> to be involved within the family.

In my fantasy, Bill Ling not only had all five cards, he "drew" a consistent "Royal Flush." In his mother's eyes he could do no wrong, and in time even Agnes would be the first to call a him a "momma's boy". Naturally prudence dictated that she only make this remark in private.

I can no longer recollect the 'hands' that were held by the rest of the family members, but I do remember that I had envisioned myself as having only two cards. Two cards! How could I ever win at this "game" with only <u>*Two*</u> cards? "I can't", I mused; "I'd have to be playing a game like blackjack or something."

"Yeah, Blackjack"

That stuck in my mind for the longest time! I continued "my game" well long after the Christmas season had past, then I forgot about it for awhile. I started to consider whether or not I was just feeling sorry for myself. "This 'game' is stupid", I thought, and just set it aside. I had not even considered taking it up again, but in time I would resume my "fantasy game", and it didn't take long.

The verbal abuse within the family was bad enough without overflowing into the workplace, but it did.

Whenever anyone other than me made a mistake on the job invariably Mom-mom's response would be something like, "Stay with it, practice makes perfect." However, if it was <u>MY</u> mistake a tirade of ridicule and put-downs would follow. Comments like, "Can't you do anything right, ya dummy?!" Oftentimes customers would be taken back by the public embarrassment that I was subjected to. Of course though, it was not their place to say anything. And of course it was especially hard for me if any of my peers happened to be in the store at the time.

In the first two months of the New Year I would continue to experience this abuse that would add ammunition to my belief that I wasn't much more to my grandmother than her 'whipping boy'.

It didn't take me long to realize that my situation would never change, and that if I wanted more than this for myself, I would have to be the one to make that change. I decided as this very young teenager that I would leave the family at my first opportunity. I was determined that I was going to have more out of life than just being the family's whipping boy.

Where does a fourteen-year-old get such insight? How did I have the awareness and ability to correctly decipher what was going on? In retrospect, I honestly believe that it was the starting of the Lord's intervention on my behalf. In many ways I have likened my treat- ment to the biblical story of Joseph. Mistreated by his family, his brothers, the scripture says; "they meant it for evil, but God meant it for good." As you will see as my story unfolds, I can certainly identify with that statement.

In the meantime I continued my 'game', playing it over and over in my mind. I then started to formulate a poem. I wrote it over and over in my head for months, massaging the information and the words. I finally put it on paper in June of 1955. I was only fifteen years old at the time that I wrote it. Here it is.

A Game of Blackjack

My family plays a poker game, oh, people can't you see. And everyone is allowed to play; everyone, of course, but me.

91

My position in the family is always in the back. But it's ok, go-ahead with your poker game; for I'm playing the game Blackjack.

Humiliations and lies to my face, and stripes upon my back. I hide my pain, I swallow my pride, and continue MY game; Blackjack

For Blackjack is the answer; and Blackjack is the key. Blackjack *wins* the poker game; the *poker* game for me!

Yes, Blackjack is the answer; and Blackjack sets me free. For Blackjack is the game of *twenty-one*; and the game belongs to me!

And there is a day that I look to, the day when I know I've won. My twenty-first birthday; January sixteenth, Nineteen-sixty-one!

That is the day that I look to; that is the day I hope for. I place the Ace and King on the table; and I turn and walk out the door.

And I have the last word, as I knew I would; and indeed that is a fact! Spoken ever so softly by me as I leave.

The final word, the Winning word; the word of course,........*Blackjack!*

I had determined in my heart and mind that I would leave; not only home but the *family*, never again to return, at the very first chance given to me. However, as you will see, the Lord had other plans for me.

Let not those who gloat over me who are my enemies without cause, let not those who hate me without reason maliciously wink the eye.

—Psalm 35:19 (NIV)

Across the street from our house on 13th and Madison, adjacent to the lake, was parkland known as "The Hollows". When I first heard the word "hollow", I didn't know what it was. I looked it up and learned that it is defined as "a small valley or basin." This aptly described the place where I would spend most of my time when I didn't want to be at home, which was practically all the time.

Whenever I wasn't in school, working at the store, or, in time, out on a date; I was over "in the hollows."

This parkland was approximately the area of three football fields; bordered by 13th Avenue, the creek that fed the lake, some houses and a tennis court, and then a B&O railroad bridge at what I considered the "back" of the property. To get to the flat, treeless basin, which was the park itself, one had to walk down an embankment, thus giving it it's appropriate name. It was all open ground, relatively smooth terrain, and an excellent place to play team sports such as baseball or football. It was also popularly used for other sports as well. My classmate, Larry Shockley, and his whole family were very much into archery. He, his parents, and older brother, could often be found on the grounds at the other end of the park practicing their sport.

Until I was sixteen years old, when I learned to drive, this is where I could be found. I liked to run; and run I did! I ran for the sheer enjoyment of it, and little by little I increased my speed. I also believe it helped me relieve some of the anguish and frustration that I was experiencing. In any case, my quickness and speed paid off in participating in my favorite sport, football. I used to enjoy playing the position of 'end', as opposed to other positions on the line. This afforded me the opportunity to use my talents, and those "covering me" on pass defense learned very quickly to "give me room", for once I got past them there was no catching me.

As I have said, I could be found there most of the time; and not at home any more than I had to be. To illustrate how intense my feelings were about this, I will give an example regarding dinner time.

Dinner was at five o'clock…Sharp! Dad was a stickler for punctuality and it was imperative that everyone had washed and groomed themselves and be at the table on time. Judy, Joan, and I, all knew that a peaceful evening centered on adhering to this rule; they were seldom late, and I never was. Actually though, this "training" in learning to be prompt would eventually serve me well, especially during the years that I would spend in the military. Still, being late was a situation to be avoided because "dad" could be very unreasonable when it came to discipline.

So, I would come home from school, change my clothes and be off to the park, football in hand. All the guys from the neighborhood would show up and we would engage in a game of touch football. I always wore my watch. If it came time for the others to leave for dinner but not for me, that was okay. I would walk over to the embankment and hide myself from the view of my house by staying on the reverse side of the hill. I would stay there until "ten-'til-five", then pick up my ball and go home. I hated living there, and I wasn't alone. And, whenever I was asked where I lived, I would typically reply, "On Mad Avenue"; referring to Madison Avenue which was our postal address.

Later on, Judy would share with me she thought living there were the worst times of her teenage years. Joan disliked it because she disliked and distrusted Bill. Agnes was not happy with the marriage, but could do little about it. She had developed diabetes, and just the cost alone of treating and managing the disease made it impossible for her to leave. There were times when her pancreas would all but totally shut down, and I can recall at least two times that she went into diabetic shock and the ambulance was summoned to take her to the hospital. She felt trapped, and in reality that was probably a correct assessment of her situation. Often she would confide in us in private; saying, "I should have left him (Bill) the day after I married him!" It seemed that no one was happy there but him.

Our home at 1240 Madison was a sterile environment, almost as if we were all roommates instead of a family. There was very little warmth; any outward expression of affection was unheard of, and communication and conversation was at a minimum. Judy would express her awe at how her "sorority sisters" interacted with their parents and siblings, and wonder why she didn't experience the same. I would have a similar opinion in regards to the families of my friends, there was a noticeable difference in how their family members related to each other.

The house that Dad had built was a beautiful three bedroom rancher on a choice parcel of property; unquestionably one of the nicest houses in the borough. But unfortunately, all three of us "kids" couldn't wait to leave; none of us considered it a real "home."

I found it easy to make new friends when we first moved there. I was "the new kid on the block", and I was readily accepted by my peers. Most of the teenagers in the area were guys, and I must admit, I was hoping that there would be some good-looking girls in the neighborhood, but alas, there were none! Darn!

One of the new friendships I had made when we moved to "Mad Avenue" was with one Jimmy Montieth. Jimmy lived up the street and around the corner from us which placed him in the Borough of Ridley Park. He was one of the regular participants in our daily football games, during the season, and we formed somewhat of a close friendship. We would see each other almost every day as he was in the habit of walking his dog down to the park after school. He had a beautiful, well-groomed Collie that he would take there each and every day for it's exercise.

When I was sixteen, and had my license, I had a '49 Pontiac convertible which I would wash two-to-three times a week. As with most teenagers with their first car, I took great pride in how it looked and I would have this bronze colored car with it's white convertible top shining like glass. Agnes told me once that I was going to wash the paint down to the primer, and if I had owned the car long enough I probably would have.

One day during our 1956 Christmas break I was out working on my "wheels" when I heard the familiar voice of Jimmy calling loudly to me from off in the distance, "Yo, Gene!" He was in the process of walking his Collie, as usual, down to "The Hollows".

I looked up from my work, and not wanting to yell to him since he was still a full block away, I waved to him and waited for him to get closer. Apparently he had something of some importance to discuss with me because he yelled again, this time saying, "Hey Gene, stay there! I want to talk to you.!" I just nodded my head conveying that I understood.

When he came up to me, I greeted him, saying, "Hey Jim, what's going on?" The conversation that followed went pretty much like this:

"I have a question for you", he replied. "What are you doing New Years Eve?"

"I don't know yet; I was going to see if Mike and Pat had anything lined up. Why?"

"Do you want to go to a party?" he asked.

"Well, maybe; where is it?" I inquired.

"Down in Chichester."

"Chichester?; *Chichester!*", I exclaimed.

"Yeah, my cousin Dolly is having one." So, how about it?" he asked.

"Dolly?" I commented. "That's and unusual name."

"Yeah; anyhow, what do you say?"

"I don't know; I don't think I want to be driving to Chichester on New Years Eve. That's kind of far, isn't it?

"It's *not* far; maybe about a twenty to thirty minute drive from here, with the traffic and all", he said.

"I don't know, I would be surprised if my Dad would let me drive that far; especially since I haven't even been driving quite a year yet. You know how he is." I explained. "He's not going to want me to be on the road with all the drunks, especially *that* night!

"C'mon" Jimmy persisted. "She' gonna have an even mix of guys and girls; she's allowed to invite fourteen people." "I've gotta tell you, she's a "looker" herself." He continued, "I know there's bound to be some nice looking girls there." "She's only got to invite one more and she'll have the seven; and if you and I go we'll round out the number of guys."

"What d'ya say?" he persisted.

"I don't know.......Chichester! Geeezzz!" " I'll tell you what", I continued. "I'll ask my dad and first see what he say's; then I'll think about it, ok?" I was still trying to get out of it but I also knew that I wanted *something* to do on New Years Eve; I certainly didn't want to be home!

"Deal", he said. "Just let me know as soon as possible, Dolly needs to know real soon, ok?"

"Ok, I'll let you know as soon as I can." was my reply.

"Cool!" See ya later! He said, leaving to continue his walk.

"Later!" I responded; and our conversation was over.

I decided that night at the dinner table to "get it over with", and asked dad about going to the party. There was a long pause, with him staring at nothing in particular, as if deep in thought. Then he surprised me. His response was, "As long as you are home by one o'clock, understood?" "Ok, I said", "I'll make sure that I'm home by then." I continued, "I'm kind of surprised that you would let me, with the distance and all the drinking that night, and all." "Well", he replied. "All the party-goers won't leave right after midnight, and by the time they get on the road you're supposed to be home. See to it that you are." "I will", I said, "thanks." He just nodded his head in response.

Again, I was truly surprised that I had permission; and now I was faced with another dilemma. I still wasn't sure I wanted to go! I was hoping there would be something going on a little closer to home. As usual, though, the guys I hung out with were notorious for procrastination, and any real plans would be left until the last minute.

After putting off my decision for as long as I could, and Jimmy's continual pleading of his case, I finally decided to go along with "the sure thing", making it clear to him that it was important that we were back by 1am. There was no way that I was going to incur the wrath of my "father" by being late. Jim understood and agreed. He had an inkling of what our home life was like. There were times when He and I would be talking by my car and dad would be coming home from work. Dad never acknowledged either one of us. I had been told by other friends that they didn't feel welcome at our house. My standard reply would be, 'Well, don't feel bad. Neither do I and I live there!" This always precipitated a chuckle from them.

The New Years Eve party started at 7pm, and Jimmy hadn't lied; Dolly was a looker, and so were all the other girls! In an instant I was glad that I was there, even if Jimmy and I were more or less the "outsiders." Everyone there, except us, was from Chichester High School; Jimmy was from Ridley Park High School and I attended Interboro. Also, we were the only two seniors, everyone else was a junior.

One surprise, which we would talk about at length later, was how friendly everyone was to us. We were not used to that. In our area strangers were treated as <u>strangers</u>, until if and when the newcomers became accepted, and that took time. Most of the groups we knew of had a certain criteria in order to fit in, and were not readily receptive to newcomers. Very cliquish would be the best description.

These people were different. They seemed genuinely interested in meeting new people and it wasn't long before Jimmy and I felt like we belonged. And another thing was different. Unlike most of the parties I was used to going to, where the guys and girls initially hung out together in their own groups, these people intermingled almost immediately. It was if some of them had known each other for a long time, and perhaps they did.

For me, there was a true "ice breaker." Chichester and Interboro were great football rivals; and this soon led to a lot of good natured teasing and bragging between me and the others.

Eventually, I would manage to talk to everyone during the course of the evening. I was glad that I was at the party, I was having a good time. There was good conversation, refreshments, music, and dancing.

Naturally, sometime during the course of the evening I made a concerted effort to talk with each of the girls. There was one that particularly sparked my interest; and partly because I got the idea that it might be reciprocated. Her name was Margie, and it seemed as if whenever I was talking with one of the other girls I would catch her watching me. As the evening wore on we would increasingly spend more time together, talking and dancing.

It seemed all too soon that we all said goodbye to the final minutes of 1956. We turned on the TV to watch the ball fall in Times Square and proclaim the arrival of a new year—1957. There were the traditional whoops and hollers, employment of noise makers, some hand shakes, and a few kisses. Then it was all over; both the celebrating and, for Jim and I, the party.

At about 12:30 am. I made the announcement that Jim and I would have to "hit the road". I used the excuse to cover what the others thought to be an early departure by saying that I had to go to work in the morning, which I did. Of course, I didn't want to reveal that I had a curfew imposed on me, it would have been embarrassing ; at least at that age I thought so. Here were the two seniors having to be home before all the juniors did, regardless of the consideration of the travel distance.

By the time we were leaving I had not even indicated to "this" Margie that I was at all interested in seeing her again, I neither asked her for a date or even her phone number. I guess in the back of my mind I was reluctant to be traveling the distance down to Chichester just for a date. Besides, I was used to pursuing any potential dates much closer to home. We teenagers lived in a time when there was a school dance at almost any school every Friday or Saturday night. I usually attended the ones at St. Gabriel's in Norwood, or Holy Cross which were much closer to home. I attended these dances regularly; but one other school also had dances, my own, Interboro, which I refused to participate in. There was a reason for that.

I started wearing glasses in sixth grade, and it was very "un-cool" for anyone to have to wear corrective vision in the era that were the '50s. It simply was not at all readily accepted by ones peers as it is today. Today, it is much easier for young people; perhaps it is because teenagers now-a-days are more mature in their thinking, or there is more prevalence of younger people wearing them. Also, the vast variety in the styles may be a factor; not to mention the availability of contact lenses which were unheard of in the '50's.

I have had conversations with numerous people that grew up in those times who experienced this same kind of mild discrimination. One of those persons is my wife; she also wore glasses during that time period and claims that she had few dates because of it. She says that it may well be a factor why she wasn't asked to attend her senior prom. The attitude of rejection was not merely psychological for those times, it was a real experience. Added to that the widespread existence of the "cliques" it was even more difficult to "fit in."

When I had embarked on the dating scene, I had asked a number of girls from my school, many of them members of my class, for a date. I have lost count of the number of times that I was specifically told , "Sorry, I don't go out with guys that wear glasses." Rejection! Thus, I started a practice of not asking out any of the girls at my school. It would become a standard policy of mine. I reasoned that I could handle the rejection, it was all part of the game, but I wasn't going to be reminded of it on a daily basis when passing these girls in the hallways on our way to our next class. A pity, because there was one particular girl that I had a "crush" on since Junior High.

She sat directly behind me in one of my math classes, but by the time I was willing to try it "just one more time" I had already attended the New Years party. Unknown to me at the time, that event would change everything, and my involvement with my own class was history.

101

About two weeks had passed when Jimmy suggested that we go down to the roller skating rink in Chester known as The Great Leopard. I had been there several times before, a great place to go, and a great place to meet girls.

We had not been there twenty minutes when in walked four people with four familiar faces. There was Dolly, with her boyfriend Bill, the girl that Jimmy had met at the party (I have long since forgotten her name), and Margie. I got the distinct feeling that this was a "set-up." In any case, I was glad to see her again, and once more, we ended up spending a lot of the evening's time together.

Before this "unofficial date" was over with, I had relented from my previous stand and asked her out. Her immediate response was a somewhat emphatic 'yes', accompanied with what I perceived to be a half-grin and half-smile, as if to be saying to herself, "Yes!, Success!" (women can be very devious!)

We dated the very next week which commenced what would become a very long relationship; with a girl I met at a party I didn't want to go to.

We both seemed to have such a good time on our first date that I asked her for another one. Again, she agreed, but instead of going out she suggested that I come for dinner and then spend the evening at home. She explained that she wanted to see me again but it wasn't necessary to go out and spend money on a date just because we wanted to be with each other. I wasn't too sure about his proposal. I had already met her parents, Harold and Verna, and they seemed nice enough; but I didn't know if I really wanted to spend the better part of an evening with them, at least not at this point.

Somewhat reluctantly, I agreed, and as it was, it proved to be a very interesting experience.

On the night of our date, shortly after I arrived, her mother asked us to come to the table and be seated. After we sat down, she instructed all of us to go ahead and "fix our plates", which we did. I took this to be the signal to go ahead and eat, and as I proceeded to do so, I could feel Margie placing her hand on my forearm as if to say, "wait!" It was then that her mother said, "Harold, would you ask the blessing?"

I was embarrassed, but it was totally unexpected. Oh, I was familiar with "saying Grace", even though it was never practiced at home, not even on special occasions like Christmas or Easter. I often witnessed it done whenever I was with my Irish friends across the street, the difference was thanks was given *before* any food was served to the plates, and not after.

I wondered if I was getting involved with a very 'religious' family, and I didn't know how I was going to fare. I didn't want to seem to be ignorant, and I certainly didn't want to be rude. I decided to "be cool" and wait for Margie's lead. My apprehension was all for naught, though, apparently her parents didn't think anything of it.

Then a whole new experience! We talked! Not polite talk, but we started to indulge in real conversations; an exchange of opinions and ideas. How novel! Something that was altogether new to me, for it was unheard of at home. Opinions weren't encouraged at the house on "Mad" Avenue.

We talked about current events, my family, her family, school, my job at the store, and a host of other subjects.

I was enjoying myself, and the fact there were people willing to listen to what I had to say. These were the first encounters of any real dialogue between me and any adults, and I found it to be a totally new experience. For me, or for that matter, Judy or Joan, to be asked about our viewpoints on any subject at home was totally inconceivable.

Slowly, Margie and I started seeing more of each other, and after about two months time I guess one would say that we had reached boyfriend-girlfriend status. I now had met most of her family.

She had three sets of Aunts and Uncles that all lived within a five block radius of her home. And, yes, they were 'religious", probably my first experiences with professing Christians.

It was not unusual at family gatherings to stand around the piano after dinner and sing hymns while Margie played. I felt extremely uncomfortable at first, but soon became used to it. I probably felt uneasy because I never liked to sing; I have not been gifted with a melodious voice. Even today I claim that the only time I get the urge to sing is when there is a full moon. I don't know if that is an indication that I have some sort of a problem or not.

I started attending church on a regular basis. Margie switched from attending the morning service to the evening one so that we could go together. Slowly, I was finding out that I enjoyed doing this, not just to be with her, but there was developing a spark of interest in the messages from the pulpit. The one thing it did was to start fostering questions about 'religion' that I had never entertained before. There were times when I would think about pursuing these questions to see if I could find some answers, but invariably I would just let the interest slip away. I now know it was the continuation of the Holy Spirit's persistent, unrelenting efforts to bring me to Christ.

There was one particular event that still today is unmistakably embedded in my mind.

The entire message at one of the Sunday evening services at the Marcus Hook Baptist Church centered solely on what it meant to be "saved." It was the very first time that I had clearly explained to me God's plan of salvation through personal faith in Jesus Christ. In retrospect, as a Christian, I think it tragic that so many churches get caught up in their own denominational "doctrine" and neglect the true Gospel message.

I listened intently to the sermon after which there was an "alter call." I can vividly remember feeling extremely uncomfortable to the point where there was *literally* sweat running down my back! Part of me wanted to go forward and part of me was embarrassed to do so. I was half afraid that it might be construed as just an act on my part, lacking any real sincerity. The truth is, there *WAS* a very real struggle going on inside me and I didn't know what to do with it. Unfortunately, I let the opportunity pass on by.

Because of pride, I had deliberately let the chance to come to Christ slip away. It could have been the last circumstance in which the Lord would give me a chance to be saved. But it wasn't! Praise God, it wasn't! Unrealized by me, He would continue to pursue me. There would still be numerous times in the future for a 'second chance', and I now find it unnerving to consider the con- sequences of dying before this "Hound Of Heaven" 'caught me' and brought me to Christ.

Even though we attended the Baptist Church in Marcus Hook, the family itself was not Baptist. As a matter of fact, I don't think they had any permanent affiliation with any particular church. A case in point would be that we also attended the Linwood Methodist Church, and on occasion, other churches. The one constant is that the churches had to Bible believing and Christ centered. Their stand seemed to be that no one denomination had 'the inside track'; they thought that the 'fine print' issues that they (the different denominations) put between themselves were petty, and detracted from the central message of the Gospel. Margie's mother would say, "the thief on the cross who acknowledged Christ didn't have a chance to join a church."

As our relationship grew, I realized that I liked being with Margie and her family. It was such a relaxed atmosphere, a place where I was more at home than *at home*! There was no air of con- tinual tension like there was on "Mad Avenue". Did they always get along? Of course not! I was witness to an occasional rift between their family members, but there was never any nastiness or vindictiveness practiced towards each other. The conflict was dealt with, and over with. Never did I witness a continuation of resentfulness or bitterness, and certainly not alienation between people. These people knew how to say their piece, and then be at peace with each other. There was never any doubt of love and acceptance for any member of Margie's family.

How different! I remember thinking, "Now, here's *a real family!*

We continued as a couple and became more focused entirely on each other and not dating anyone else. Then came the month of May, the month that "Mother's Day" is celebrated; a day in which *every year* I would wonder where our mom was but could never find out.

It was on this Mother's Day, 1957, during a conversation at their dinner table that her parents asked me about my plans after graduation. I indicated that my immediate plans were to enlist in the Air Force. I explained that college held no interest for me, at least for the time being; I felt as if I had enough of school for awhile, and it was for certain I wasn't waiting for the Army to draft me.

They listened to my plans and acknowledged their understanding and then we moved on to other conversations.

106

Nothing more was said on the subject, that is, (apparently) until after I had left for the evening.

On our next date Margie revealed to me that her parents had determined that she and I could write to each other while I was away in the service, but that we should no longer consider ourselves to be a 'couple'. They reasoned that we were too young, which we were, and it was unfair for both of us to consider not dating or having a social life apart from each other.

Unknown to them, we had already discussed this subject between the two of us and had come to the same conclusion. We agreed to write to each other regularly and when I was home 'on leave' we would spend our time together. And, as 'fate' would have it, that is pretty much the way things would play out.

Four weeks later I was in Texas, in basic training, in the Air Force.

> I know, O Lord, that a man's life is not his own; it is not for man to direct his steps.
> —Jeremiah 10:23 (NIV)

CHAPTER SEVEN

AIR FORCE

SAC

For as long as I can remember I have always been interested in aircraft. Actually, fascinated would be the proper word.

There was a period of time from when I was about age 13 to 16 that it was not unusual for me to ride my bicycle over to the Philadelphia Airport to watch the planes. It was always on a Saturday, after my chores were done, that I would fill my World War II canteen with water, attach it to its corresponding web belt, and head off for the airport five miles away. It should be noted that this was a perfectly safe thing to do; in a time when one could go much of anywhere they desired without fear of someone bothering them. How times have changed.

The only thing I had to make sure of is that I was home at a reasonable time to avoid any suspicion as to where I had gone and what I was doing. I knew that it would not have been approved of so I just didn't tell anyone what I had been up too. One of those private "sneaky" moments we are all probably guilty of; at one time or another. If asked what I had been doing all day I would just reply, "Just out riding my bike". It wasn't a lie, but it wasn't the whole truth either.

Philadelphia Airport was considerably smaller then, the 50's, and there was an observation deck over the terminal that was open to the general public; one only had to climb the staircase to get to it.

I would spend all day there watching the planes take off and land, totally engrossed, practically oblivious of anything else going on around me. "Lunch" would consist of anything the vending machines had to offer and there was always a fountain nearby whenever I had to replenish my water supply. The only concern I had was to make sure that I kept checking my watch so to make certain I got back home in a timely manner.

My interest in airplanes was such that I was familiar with almost all of the World War II aircraft, both allied and axis. I often thought if I had been a grown-up during the war years I would have been a good "spotter". I could always identify the aircraft illustrated on the silhouette cards that were in use during that time.

So, coupled with the promise to myself I would leave home at the first opportunity, the Air Force was the most logical choice for me in which to fulfill my military obligation. The draft was still in effect at the time and I didn't want to wait to hear from the Army; a letter that usually starts with the ominous word, "Greetings".

I joined the Air Force right after graduation from high school. Judy and I graduated together on June 7th and I was in basic training at Lackland Air Force Base on June 14th. I was inducted into the military at the post office in Chester and then boarded a bus that would take me and the other enlistees to Philadelphia for our flight to Texas.

I recall looking out the window at Bill, Agnes, and Judy just as the bus was leaving and thinking, "You may never see me again". Indeed, that had been my original plan, but now I had a tremendous struggle going on inside me. Part of me said, "Remember, you aren't leaving home, you're leaving the *family!*". But now things were a little more complicated, due to that "woman" in Chichester; the one I met at a party that I didn't want to go to. I knew, even then, she would be the only possible reason I might return. Still, I struggled, the desire to break my ties with the family was incredibly strong. It would be a good many years and not before I became a Christian that I would understand how all this was to play out, and the reason behind it; and to understand the scripture that says, "Many are the plans in a man's heart, but it is the Lord's purpose that prevails". (Proverbs 19: 21 NIV)

Basic training in any branch of our Armed Forces can be best described by two simple words; organized harassment.

"Boot camp", as it is often called, may be more intense in some of the branches of our military than others, the Marine Corps for example, but all of it is an acute adjustment from the norm; and to the uninformed most of the harsh treatment seems to be ridiculous and unnecessary. But it is necessary; very necessary.

I was billeted in a barracks with 63 other enlistees; people from all walks of life, a conglomeration of ethnic, racial, economic, and social backgrounds. The TI's (training instructors, as they were called in the Air Force) had six weeks to bring everyone down to the same level; even the playing field as it were. A rich kid from Chicago might find himself cleaning the latrine alongside another enlistee from a poverty stricken family in Mississippi. There were no class distinctions, no connections, no advantages or privileges afforded to anyone. We were all "in the same jar", airmen basic, and your background meant nothing. The shredding of one's individualism was complete, and the military way of doing things thoroughly instilled.

There was the trip to "The Green Monster", a large green hangar where we would receive our clothing issue. The first thing given to us was a duffel bag in which all of our uniforms that would be our wardrobe for the next four years would be crammed into.

Next would be the medics. Blood would to drawn and typed; information needed to be permanently etched onto our dog tags. Then the shots. We single filed between two medics perched on stools with trays of syringes located within their easy reach. Both of them would pick up a syringe in each hand and, Bam!, four injections all at once!! Great fun!

There was PT, KP, guard duty and marching. Also classes on military etiquette, military regulations, command structure, and the Code of Conduct; the instruction that dealt with the subject of being a POW; and marching.

There was weapons training, gas mask training, bivouacs, and marching. There were barrages of aptitude tests to determine what talents you might possess and how the Air Force might best utilize them; and there was marching. Oh, did I mention that there was a lot of marching?

On the Monday of the last week two other airmen and I were informed by our TI that we were to report to the First Sergeant at "thirteen-hundred hrs." (1pm.), and "you will be there!" was his remark of "encouragement".

We were subsequently informed by the sergeant that all of us had an appointment at the base headquarters building the next day. He said, "You are to report at ten-hundred hrs. (10am), and you will be there"! More encouragement!

Some things in the Air Force were consistent, and the phrase "You will be there!" was one of them.

No one would tell us what it was all about and our imagination shifted into high gear. Were they kicking us out? Were we being assigned to some cloak and dagger ops? Were we being charged with espionage? What?!!

All of us reported to headquarters on time, of course; only to wait another hour (of course) before we knew why we were there.

The three of us were to have an interview, in turn, with three officers; a 1st Lieutenant, a Captain, and a Major. We would learn that these officers were from the OSI , Office of Security Investigations, the security branch of the Air Force that conducts background checks.

In my case, I had been investigated by the 9th OSI District operating out of Philadelphia. I was in the process of being given a Top Secret security clearance, necessary to the career I was to have during my four years in the Air Force. I was being sent to the Air Force Communications School at F. E. Warren A.F.B. outside Cheyenne, Wyoming. We were informed during an indoctrination meeting, which included other airmen headed for various specialized schools; "No one sets foot through the door of these schools without such a clearance, no one is going to learn anything about these fields without one. Also, you people will end up taking on responsibilities you probably don't want; *we don't care,* you got'em anyhow! The Air Force has your 'butt' (not the word he used) for the next four years." Then he started using the "we will's and you will's". "WE WILL use you the way we want to! YOU WILL be _properly_ trained, and YOU WILL do your duty! YOU WILL do your duty, or WE WILL send your sorry 'butt' (still not the word he used!) to Leavenworth! Understood?" "Sir, Yes Sir!" was our reply in unison.

After this brief speech to give us the *incentive* to excel in the tasks we were to perform for the next four years was completed; and after our interviews with these three officers was finished, we were then dismissed back to our individual training squadrons. I would find out later that the other two airmen being interviewed had other assignments.

One was going to the Air Police School; and the other airman to the Nuclear Ordinance (weapons) School. He would become part of the ground crews that armed our bombers with their two nuclear bombs in the bomb-bays, and a nuclear tipped "Hound-dog" missile with a range of 600 miles affixed under each wing of the huge Boeing B-52's.

Part of the purpose of the interview was to review and perhaps confirm much of the information that had been collected. They knew everything!

They conducted a two generation background check on my "parents". They knew who my friends were; their family's background and political affiliations. They knew who Judy was dating, Bernard Keenan, and <u>his</u> background. They also knew my teachers, places I frequented, my girl-friend Margie (and her parents background), plus a host of other "info."

Then it came, the comment! The Major made the state-ment, "Oh, and I see that you were adopted." It was the first time I had heard the word and it didn't connect. I don't know if it was the pressure of basic training, my age (17), or the fact that I just wanted the interview to be over. In any case, I didn't give the statement any credibility. I thought, "Well, they got it right so far but this is really bogus!" I blurted out, "Adopted! What do you mean adopted? I wasn't adopted!" Then I immediately thought I might be in trouble for abruptly ignoring military protocol and not properly addressing my superior. But I wasn't, nothing was said about my sudden outburst.

It was then the Major realized that I didn't know about being adopted and quickly moved on past the subject.

It would be another seven years, at age 24, before I would find out that it was indeed the truth. I never in my wildest dreams ever thought that might have been the case. Judy, however, had been suspicious since we were fourteen.

It was right after Dad had built his house on Madison Ave. and we were in the process of moving from Mom-moms to our new home. As usual, in a move, things are in disarray and many things are packed quickly without much thought. In my room I had a desk with a typewriter on it and Judy was in the process of typing something for school and needed more paper. She opened one of the drawers to the desk and there they were, adoption papers. Unfortunately she didn't get a good chance to exam them as Dad and Agnes were pulling into the driveway. She quickly closed the drawer and proceeded with her typing. Dad must have then realized how close Judy was, let's say, "to the truth", as he had apparently removed the documents later at his first opportunity. The next time Judy had a chance to check on them they were gone. She did not share her discovery with me until many years later. She had been afraid that if I knew I would have probably run away from home. I'm not at all sure she was wrong.

The flight from Lackland to Cheyenne was aboard a C-47, a "gooney-bird", one of the work horse aircraft of the military. This was the type of aircraft best known for its role in the Normandy invasion on D-Day; having dropped hundreds of "sticks" of paratroopers behind the German defensive positions on the coast that would become known as "The Atlantic Wall". Some aviation historians have claimed that the C-47 was the sturdiest, most reliable aircraft ever built.

Communications school was all encompassing; anything that had to with that field was taught there; telephone, radio, and teletype operators; linemen, maintenance, instrument repairmen, etc. Absolutely everything! I can still visualize one parade ground peppered with the tallest telephone poles I had ever seen; and watch the linemen practice climbing up and down them; using their harness belts around the waist and the spikes which were attached to their boots that dug into the poles as they climbed.

As for me, I would become a Communications Center Specialist (teletype operations), and the course was eleven weeks long.

Military schools are like none other, there is no non-sense. We would actually march to school, marching single file into the classroom and stand at attention beside our assigned desks.

There was complete silence. We would be seated only when the instructor commanded, "Sit down!" With a re-sounding reply of "Yes, Sir!" we would take our seats and immediately class would begin.

The course was extensive and difficult, with much material to cover in eleven weeks. I felt overwhelmed and apprehensive, and my confidence was sinking. I thought perhaps I was in over my head. After all, I was always told that I was a dummy; I couldn't do anything right. I had to fight the memories of being repeatedly told, "You aren't worth a tinker's dam, and you'll never amount to anything!" I wanted to do well but I wasn't sure that I could. Neverthe-less, I would give it my best shot. What else could I do?! I couldn't get out of it so the only option was to try hard and hope for the best.

At the end of the eleven weeks there would be a final exam. Those who passed would be given a fifteen-day furlough, after which they would move on to their next assignment. The base they reported to would start their career in earnest.

Those that failed, the term was called "phased back", had to repeat the course. If they again failed they would be reassigned to another "less demanding" school, perhaps "Food Service" or something else.

I studied *hard*.

My incentive was twofold. First, and most importantly, I wanted to prove to myself that I had what it took to succeed and pass this course. Secondly, I had admitted to myself I did want to return "home", but only because I was developing a growing interest in Margie.

The final exam was in two parts, a written exam and a typing exam. I had two years of typing as an elective in high school so I was not overly concerned about that part of the test. My real concern was with the written part, there was just *so much* material to cover!

The test consisted of six pages of questions, on both sides, and one-and-a- half hours to answer them, plus the typing. Not a lot of time, but the position of the instructors was that either you knew the material or you didn't!

The two days to get the results were stressful for all of us, after all, everyone one at this point had enough of "basic" and we wanted to get to our duty stations and start "being in the Air Force".

The test results were posted on the barracks bulletin board, and everyone crowded around to find out how they did. The posting was in two sections, those that passed in the first and those who phased back in the second. There we were, sixty-four airmen trying to get a glimpse of what the immediate future held in store for each of us.

I scanned the list of those that had passed and my heart sank; my name was not there!

I panicked!! Again, I checked it! Two, three times I checked it! My name was *not* listed under those who passed. With extreme anxiousness and frustration I fought the impulse to reveal how upset I was. Reluctantly, my eyes wandered down to the list of those who phased back.

Again, my name was not there! By this time we were standing there about five deep in front of the board and, thinking out loud, I said, "I can't find my name". Then I heard someone off to my right say, "Hey Ling, it's at the top of the page, all the way up at the top".

It was a special recognition; I had a *perfect* exam!

It took a few moments for my mind to process what had just happened and what it was telling me. Then the light went on. The light that the cartoonist draws over the head of one of his characters denoting revelation and understanding.

For the absolutely *very first time in my life* I realized that I was not stupid! I finally saw myself as one with talents to be nurtured and cultivated, and the realization that I was not the "dummy" I had so often been told that I was. *It was a pivotal point in my life*. It would set a whole new direction in how I viewed myself, after seeing a glimpse of the true person that I was.

I fought back the tears, I didn't want anyone to see how upset I was; I knew that they would never understand. But they were not tears of joy, they were tears of anger!! All the putdowns, all the sarcasm; the hurt and rejection, overflowed my memory all at one time. Lies! They were all lies! I wondered just how many other lies I had been told. In time, Judy and I would find out there were many.

Then came the accolades, the congratulations, the "atta boys", and all from strangers, and a thousand miles from home.

It would be several hours before the anger subsided. Then a sense of peace and satisfaction came over me. It was a new revelation to me, a sense of accomplishment that I had never experienced before. I finally knew the truth about myself, and I was embarking on a new journey. From that day forward, October 23, 1957, I would be rebuilding my sense of self-worth I had been stripped of in my childhood, and I would never again allow anyone to attack my intellect.

The next day we individually received our written orders for our next assignment. I was going to the Strategic Air Command, our nuclear bomber forces. It was well known that SAC, as it was called, got the *top ten percent* of the graduates from *all* the Tech Schools within the Air Force, and only the <u>best</u> of those were assigned to a <u>headquarters</u> unit.

My orders read that I was to report to the 46th Communications Squadron, 2nd Bomb Wing, Headquarters 2nd Air Force, Strategic Air Command; at Barksdale A.F.B., Shreveport, LA.

But first, I was going home.

"Because of the oppression of the weak and the groaning of the needy, I will now arise," says the Lord. "I will protect them from those who malign them."

—Psalm 12:5 (NIV)

119

The "Lucky" Airman

Living out of Cheyenne; F. E. Warren is the spot.
We were doomed forever; in a land that God forgot.
Living with the sergeants; living where the men are blue.
Right in the middle of nowhere; and a very long way from you.
We sweat, burn, and itch; it's more than men can stand.
We're not really convicts; just defenders of our land.
We are hard working people; all for our measly pay.
Guarding people with millions; for only $2.50 a day.
Living with our memories; just waiting to see our gal.
Hoping that while we're away; she hasn't married my pal.
Nobody knows we're living; nobody gives a damn.
At home we're all forgotten; for we belong to "Uncle Sam."
Now, when we get to heaven; Saint Peter we will tell.
"We're airmen from Warren, Sir; and we've spent our time in
hell."
So, to you who are free today; please take heed from this.
If the draft doesn't get you, for goodness sake, don't enlist!
Gene Ling
3457th Student Squadron
Francis E. Warren Air Force Base
Cheyenne, Wyoming

It has just been too long ago!

I'm not even sure of the years, other than they were sometime in the early 50's. . On one particular day our teacher was giving us a "pop quiz" when the fire alarm sounded. The school district was required to practice two fire drills sometime during the school year. Our drills were usually conducted with one in the Fall and one in the Spring.

On this occasion, when the bell sounded, those students seated in the row closest to the windows scurried to huddle tightly against the wall underneath them. Everyone else was instructed to quickly clear their desks and position themselves as best they could under them. In addition, we were to take the heaviest book we had and cover our face and neck to protect them from the shards of glass that was sure to engulf the classroom, precipitated by the shock wave from the nuclear blast.

This was not a fire drill; it was an air raid drill!

It was the early part of an era that would become known as "the cold war". The principal countries involved were the Soviet Union and the United States, with much finger shaking and "saber rattling" between them. The distrust between our two countries escalated and so did the arms race. A nuclear attack by the Soviet Union was a real possibility, if not a probability, and our leaders deemed it necessary to prepare for such an eventuality. Perhaps the fiasco of Pearl Harbor was still fresh in their minds.

"Nike" antiaircraft missile batteries, operated by the Army, were positioned around our major cities and industrial centers. Chester, Pa. had two such installations that I know of. There were Civil Defense air raid shelters designated by special signs and the shelters were always in locations that were underground; the basement of a large building, an underground parking garage, or a subway station.

Government sponsored TV commercials were aired to inform the public what to do in case of a nuclear attack. In addition, they provided free pamphlets on instructions how to build a underground air raid shelter for ones own family. In time, I would eventually work for a chemist who actually built such a shelter in his backyard.

The animosity between our two countries was severe; best illustrated by the now famous speech given by the Soviet premier Nikita Khrushchev to the General Assembly of the United Nations in 1956. At one point in his tirade against the U.S. he removed one of his shoes and, pounding the podium with it, pointed a finger at our ambassador and screamed, "We will bury you!" Here was the leader of the second most powerful nation in the world losing control of himself in front of all the ambassadors from most of the countries of the civilized world. These, indeed, were very scary times!

The primary mission of the Strategic Air Command was to keep the peace; to have such an awesome retaliatory nuclear force that every nation would realize that a nuclear attack on the United States was not only un-winnable, but also un-thinkable. The official motto of SAC was "Peace Is Our Profession." To ensure this, it always maintained a very high state of readiness for war, undermining anyone's temptation to start one. It has been said that its attitude was similar to that of our national crest, the one found on our currency depicting the eagle with its "eyes on the olive branch, arrows at the ready".

The intercontinental ballistic missiles were not yet part of either country's arsenal and a nuclear attack would have been conducted using manned bombers and missile-laden submarines.

That being the case, SAC had over a thousand bombers stationed at over forty bases world-wide; and they were always kept in a high state of readiness. One third of the Command was on a fifteen minute ground alert at all times; and a classified number of nuclear-armed bombers were airborne 24/7. This was the posture of the Strategic Air Command from the time of the launching of the Soviet satellite "Sputnik" in October of 1957 until the collapse of the Soviet Union in December of 1991. The general public never knew that whatever they were occupied in doing during all those years there was a fleet of airborne B-52's flying overhead, each bomber armed with four nuclear weapons.

Alert exercises in Sac were the norm, conducted at least once a month and on many occasions, more. They were always unannounced and termed "ORI's". An ORI was an Operational Readiness Inspection, and the base's performance (read Base Commander's career) was under the close scrutiny of an inspection team from SAC Headquarters in Offutt, Nebraska.

We knew that all our bases were targeted by the Soviets, therefore it was paramount for the bombers to be airborne and away from the base as quickly as humanly possible. That phase of the exercise was called a MITO, or Minimum Interval Takeoff exercise.

A typical Bomb Wing in SAC consisted of three squadrons of bombers and one tanker Squadron, fifteen aircraft in each. These planes would "roll" down the runway at 12 to 15 seconds apart and the entire Wing (60 aircraft) would be launched in well under twenty minutes; something that one would never see at a commercial airport!

The aircrews always stayed together when on duty. They went to the Base Exchange, the Commissary, and the chow-hall together; they never separated. If one had to get a haircut, the entire bomber crew of six were at the barber shop. The base movie theatre had reserved seats for them next to the exit doors with the "panic" bars. The station wagons that would rush them to the flight line were parked just outside those doors. Those alert vehicles were the best maintained vehicles in the world; I have never heard of an instance when one of them would not start or broke down. As I have already stated, SAC got the best from all the schools, and that included the mechanics for the Motor Pool.

Not all the aircrews were scattered across the base. Some were on duty at the flight line itself. These crews would be the first to man their bombers and taxi into position to start the MITO sequence once the Klaxon horns, with their deafening blast, sounded the alert.

General Curtis E. LeMay was the Commander of the Strategic Air Command when I served in the late 50,s and early 60,s. Later, he would be "out of his element" when he got involved in politics, but as a strategic commander he was superb. He was well experienced in commanding large forces of military aircraft; and was instrumental in planning and conducting the strategic bombing of Japan's homeland during World War II, when the air arm of our military was still under the command of the Army Air Corps.

He would be quoted as saying "Our state of readiness is to be so that someone in the Kremlin gets up *every day*; turns to Khrushchev and says, "Today, Is <u>Not</u> the day, comrade!" He was also quoted as saying, "As long as I am Commander-in-Chief of our Strategic Air Command there will <u>never</u>, <u>ever</u>, be another Pearl Harbor."

Such was the elite military organization that I was a part of, and I am at all not embarrassed to say that I was proud to serve in it.

I decided to include this little discourse on SAC for several reasons. First, as I have already indicated, it was tremendously instrumental in rebuilding my sense of ac-complish- ment and self-worth. Secondly, I am keenly aware that there is an entire generation that is oblivious of its ex-istence and the critical role it played in maintaining world peace for four decades. And thirdly, but by no means less important, the Lord would place two individuals in my path who would share the Gospel of Jesus Christ with me.

My first duty in the Communication Center at Barksdale was to assist sending information to the dozen or so bases that were under the command of the 2nd Air Force. I would be operating a facsimile machine, the forerunner of what is now commonly known as a "Fax" machine. It was, at the time (1957-58), the only method available for transmitting photos and maps electronically.

We would receive the most updated weather maps of Eastern Europe and the Soviet Union from SAC Headquar-ters and forward them to the bases under our command.

The maps would be affixed to a "drum", then mounted on a cradle that moved from left to right. As the drum ro-tated on the cradle an electronic eye would read the image and transmit it. It would take approximately thirty minutes to send just one map; archaic by today's standards but at the time it was "state of the art".

It was a relatively simple task, an important one, as the aircrews needed to know what weather conditions they might be facing if an attack on the Soviet Union became necessary. Still, I thought, "I went to eleven weeks of school for *this*!" "Is this all I'm going to be doing?" Of course, it wasn't. I was just "getting my feet wet". In time I would work the entire scope of what a Communication Center Specialist entailed, short of becoming a supervisor. That position was more readily a function of rank than of qualifications, and was normally filled by NCOs.

The person training me in this task was a WAF (Women's Air Force) who's name was Nancy. She was an Airman 1st Class (3 stripes) and I was an Airman 3rd Class (1stripe); the stripe being awarded upon completion of basic training and Tech School. She outranked me, but then just about everyone did!

She was a good teacher, and as we worked together, and got to know each other, we became friends. In time we would share a little about our backgrounds. She was from Oklahoma and her husband was also in the Air Force and worked in administration. At one point she asked me why I had joined the Air Force so young. I replied, "Basically, just to get away from home". I never discussed anything in detail but after awhile she deduced that there were "problems at home", and my life there had been far less than what it should have been.

I can recall her saying to me, "Ling, you need to turn your life over to Jesus Christ". I would listen patiently and politely to her Gospel message and then I would push it aside. I knew that I was an angry young man and I knew in my own mind that I wasn't ready for any "religion".

Besides, I had done some Bible reading in the past and I remembered that Jesus himself had given the command to be "perfect". I reasoned that I was a "far cry" from that; so the whole thing just seemed to be totally impossible. How in the world, I thought, was I supposed to please a Holy God when I couldn't even please my parents? I just let the whole question slide.

Nancy and I worked solidly together for three months, then less so while I was being introduced to the "hands on" aspects of teletype operations. I was fascinated! The on-the-job training went smoothly and because I found it so incredibly interesting I picked up all the fine points fast. My hard work at school was paying off; not only did I know the material at school, I knew how to implement the material to its practical application. I excelled at what I did! So much so, that in another four months I was assigned to the Headquarters building itself. We had what were called "pony-circuits" located there adjacent to the war room. These were teletype circuits, over secured lines, connected directly to the main communications center. This was a security measure. This allowed all classified messages to remain within the headquarters building and eliminated the need for couriers to hand carry the messages to the communications center and possibly create a security risk.

"The Shed", as we called the communication room at headquarters was somewhat small but adequate enough to perform the duties that we were there to do. There were seven people assigned per shift; an officer, a NCO, and five enlisted men. The officer, usually a 2nd Lieutenant, was there to interact with the staff in the war room. The NCO, typically a Staff Sergeant, oversaw the performance of all the communications procedures conducted within the shed.

The responsibilities of the other five of us were shared; two "cutters" and three operators. The cutters were those who typed up the messages to be sent. While they were typing the actual message on a teletype machine a ticker-tape was being "cut" by another machine. Once the tape was made it could then be transmitted by positioning the tape in a transmitting machine, flip a switch, and "off she went" at eighty-five words a minute. "Cutters" were very good at what they did, excellent typists! We had one career airman that was so good at his craft he was known as "fingers".

"Fingers" would start cutting a tape just long enough to reach a transmitting devise; tell the operator to start sending the message, and then continue cutting the message, keeping up with the transmitter. I have personally seen him do a five page message this way, and when the message was finished being sent, the "hard copy" had no mistakes! Incredible!

Operators did exactly that; they operated the teletype machines; sending and receiving the myriad of messages, not only to the bases under our command, but also to every base within the Strategic Air Command. We were kept very busy, there was always a lot of message traffic to handle; anything from unclassified to TOP SECRET// FOR EYES ONLY. These were messages always directed to the Wing (base) Commander and an absolute minimum number of personnel were privy to the information that was in them, usually only six people. These were; the originator of the message, the one who cut tape to be sent, the operator sending, the operator receiving, the shift supervisor at the base the message was received, and the Wing Commander at that base. Six people in the whole world knew what the message said; and four of them were in Communication Operations. In a way, it was quite an honor to be entrusted with such a position; and I was starting to feel good about myself, a feeling that was long overdue.

The most interesting message that I would personally receive during my Air Force career (unclassified) was from our SAC base in Guam. I happened to be the one operating the teletype when the message stated that a Japanese soldier from WWII had just surrendered after hiding out for fifteen years. His name was Ito Musashi, who would subsequently tell his story in a book titled, "The Emperor's Last Soldiers". And, of course, this book is part of my library on military history.

We all had our turn working "the shed". Most of the time it was the same crew, rotating in turn with others.

Our sergeant in charge was a Staff Sergeant Bowers, and he would be the second person to witness to me.

I didn't know Sgt. Bowers before he became a Christian and I probably wouldn't have wanted to. His past reputation was one of a drunkard and womanizer. It was well known that after receiving his pay from the Paymaster he would head for the bars and "honky-tonks" lining both sides of the main roads through Bossier City, just outside the base's main gate. If payday happened to be during a time he didn't have to report for duty, he would do his carousing until his money was almost spent. He would be gone from home for days. It got so bad that his wife had to have his pay "attached" so as to make sure she had enough funds to run their household.

But now he was different, and if one had not known him before, when this was all happening, you wouldn't believe they were talking about the same person. Now, he was a very laid-back, gentle, and soft spoken person. He was the personification of an individual who was "a new creature in Christ". The only time he might get a little loud was when he would sporadically burst out with a "Thank you, Jesus!", or "Praise the Lord!" The Lord had changed him drastically, and he was very enthusiastic about sharing how that change came about; and his relationship with God through faith in Jesus Christ. He witnessed to everyone; and of course, I had my turn. And, *of course*, I wasn't "buying it".

Sgt. Bowers was a more than a capable supervisor. He was unquestionably the most knowledgeable communications supervisor that I have ever worked for during my entire service career. There didn't seem to be any communications problem or situation that he couldn't handle, and he rarely consulted the three large manuals we used for directions. And, when it came to the code book (about the size of a telephone book) he seemed to know what codes to use without looking them up. His memory was nothing short of phenomenal, and we all swore he had the book memorized!

As an operator, your job entailed that you move around; to be seated when responsible for working with multiple teletype machines was not practical. Therefore, the machines were mounted on top of consoles. These consoles were at the height which made it easy to both type and read the hard copies that were being sent or received.

They would be positioned so that the operators would be, in many cases, facing each other. Mine were positioned so that I could see our supervisor at his desk, and it seemed that whenever Sgt. Bowers wasn't involved with a communication problem, he was either praying or reading his Bible.

Every once in a while he would shout out one of his, "Praise the Lord", or, "Thank you Jesus" exclamations. Some of my fellow workers, who had their backs to him, would roll their eyes or stifle a snicker in mockery. I never did. I thought to do so was to perhaps make fun of God as much as him. Quite frankly, and somewhat surprisingly, I was afraid to. And on one occasion I can remember specifically looking at him in wonderment and thinking, asking myself, "Who's to say it isn't so?"

I can also recall thinking, "What's going on here! Every time I turn around someone's talking "religion" to me. It seemed to me like I was being "hounded."

Exactly!

And the "hound of heaven" wasn't done with me yet!

Many are the plans in a man's heart, but it
is the Lord's purpose that prevails.
—Proverbs 19:21 (NIV)

Bill and Betty Ling
Judy and Me

Mom-mom and Pop-pop

618 Summit Avenue

Dad", Judy and Me
Living at "Mom-mom's"
after the divorce.

131

1240 "Mad" Avenue.

Agnes and Bill
Wedding day, 1948.

Agnes and Joan
Cottage at Crystal Beach.

Judy and Me
Crystal Beach, 1956

Carol and Me

Our sons, Gary, Matt and Mike
(l. to r.)

Mom and husband Paul Jump
Judy and me

Gregg and Patty

Family Reunion
Gary, Carol, Me, Judy, Mom, Gregg, and Patty

Mom with grandsons Mike (l.) and Matt (r); and great-grandson Josh.

Cousin Lana, Aunt Esther, and Me.

Our birthplace, Crozer Hospital for
the Incurables

"The Twins"
Me (l.), Judy (r.)

Our parents,
Eugene Carroll Hall and Theodora
(Dora) Killen Hall

Our Mother with Judy (l.) and Me (r.)

CHAPTER EIGHT

DOWNTURN

SPIRALING DOWN... DOWN...DOWN

Not all the graduates of my squadron from the Air Force Communications School were given stateside bases as their first assignment after graduation. Clearly one-third of my classmates would start their Air Force careers overseas.

Because of this, there was a standard policy that those whose destinations where our bases were on "foreign soil", would be given a 30-day furlough, or leave, before having to report to the military terminals which would provide transportation to their next duty station. These typically were McGuire A.F.B., New Jersey, for those headed for Europe; and Travis A.F.B. in California for those traveling to our bases in the Pacific. Included in the installations designated as "overseas" were our bases in Alaska, and Hickam A.F.B. in Hawaii. These were included in that category because of the distance of those assign- ments from the "lower 48", and the time and expense it would take an airman to plan a trip home.

Everyone else that had been given orders to report to a base in the "continental" United States, which included me, were given a 15-day leave.

Travel expenses from the military is only provided from your current duty station to your next. For me, this meant that I would receive travel pay to get me from Wyoming to Shreveport, Louisiana; and as far as the military was concerned I had 15 days to get there. If I wanted to go anywhere else in the interim the expense would be on me.

We had been informed of this regulation beforehand and everyone seemed to be astute enough to save enough funds from their pay to afford a ticket home. On one of our weekend passes, a group of us headed for the airport in Cheyenne to make our individual travel arrangements, and I made mine for Philadelphia.

One of the conversations that we would have in the barracks in the previous weeks was trying to figure out when we would have a chance to return home to see family. The guys would talk about being anxious to return for awhile, they missed their loved ones dearly. Some had never been away from home for any length of time before, and they were truly homesick. The question they posed to themselves was, "I wonder when I'll get a chance to go home?" My dilemma was not figuring out the answer to that question, but rather trying to answer the one, "Why would I want to?"

I was being perfectly honest with myself. My reason for returning was to see my girlfriend, and not much more than that. I figured that I would find out shortly if we would pick up our relationship where we had left off, or if I could read whether or not it it had cooled from Margie's standpoint. I really had nothing to lose as I could always continue on to my assignment anytime during that period of furlough. The orders read, "on or about" a certain date, which meant that one could sign into the squadron at anytime during that period. They would only be charged for the leave time actually used. The only thing critical was they must report by the end of the final day, or they would be considered AWOL, or "absent without leave"; a poor way to start one's service career.

Since Margie had faithfully written to me two to three times a week, I presumed there was a definite interest on her part in wanting to see me again. After all, if not, she could have sent me one of those dreaded "Dear John" letters. She had not. Others in the barracks had gotten such mail, but I was not one of them. So, I would give it a try; and in the last week of October I was on my way to "Philly."

I was true to the personal vow that I had made to alienate myself from the family. I was more than willing to continue my relationship with my girlfriend; but in no way was I going to permit myself to allow my home life to pick up where we left off. I was done with the abuse. I spent twelve of the fifteen day leave with Margie and her entire family. As it would turn out, there would be only three days that I would not be down in Chichester visiting them.

One was to honor an agreement with my friends.

We had a pact, that, if possible, we would all try to return to the area at the same time during the Fall. As destiny would have it, it worked out almost perfectly. Only one, Ed Acker, who was in the Marines, was the sole person missing.

We planned that sometime during our leave time home we would all get together for a pickup game of touch football; with the understanding the losers would be the ones responsible for the half-keg of beer. With that at stake, we all played very hard. Unfortunately, my team lost!

The second time was at a family dinner. Even at that, my girlfriend was with me. It was at Mom-moms, with eleven of the usual twelve present. Our step-sister Joan was was now married to Jack, and she and her husband were now living in Hawaii. He was also in the Air Force and was stationed at Hickam. Margie was now taking Joan's place at the table.

One thing that was very noticeable about that evening was that only Judy and our aunt Bernice took any interest in my experiences. They were the only two who seemed curious as to what I would be doing in the Air Force, where I would be going, or what bacic training was like. Typical!

By contrast, Margie's family couldn't find out enough. They were very much interested in my experiences and what I would be doing. They wanted to know what the schooling was like and asked many questions about it. Naturally, there were times I would have to side-step their inquiries because of security reasons. We had already been advised as to what questions and answers where strictly "off limits."

It should be noted that my girlfriend was still in school, a senior at Chichester. Most of each day we were not together. Still, I preferred to be with her family rather than my own.

The final day of my leave would be a travel day. I would be in transit to the base that would start my career.

This little scenario that I have just described would be repeated essentially the same throughout my service experience. Any of the time that I spent at home would be sparsely designated. I have since long ago calculated how much time I actually spent with my own "family" when I was on leave and came up with a menial six days out of seventy-seven. All the other time was allotted between my girlfriend and friends.

It was during the last leave that I would take in the military that my grandmother could no longer be silent as to how I was spending my time. She was angry, and she showed it. On one brief encounter she angrily barked at me, "All you do is spend all your time with those damn Alexander's!" (Margie's family name).

"Well, Mom-mom", I replied, "That's because I've found there what I have never been able to find at home."

"Well, what's that?" she retorted.

"Acceptance", I answered; "They like me."

"Hrummp!", "Well, they don't know you the way I know you!" she sarcastically responded.

My rebuttal to that was, "No, Mom-mom; that's the point, you don't know me at all!" "I'm not who you say that I am!" Nothing! Not a single word.

She just didn't seem to know what to say. It was as if she had been found out; I had let her know that I realized what was going on, and it wasn't going to work anymore. The days of the guilt trips and character assassinations were over with. No more "whipping boy" status for me. I think that it finally sank in, for after that exchange I noticed an all new level of respect towards me. Our relationship would begin to change, not close, but certainly better than it had been.

Also, something else had changed during my last time home on leave. It was obvious to Margie and me, and her parents as well, that our relationship had evolved past the "boyfriend-girlfriend" stage, and we were now very much serious about each other.

I asked her to marry me in February of 1960, and she very enthusiastically accepted my proposal. Her parents were not at all surprised, and gave us their blessing. They were keenly aware as to how our involvement had progressed; had witnessed it develop over the years, becoming apparent to them that we had developed this intense relationship. Their only concern now was that Margie and I would not make any marriage plans until she was finished with her education. She was now out of high school and attending Temple University, and finishing college was extremely important to both her and her parents.

I had no problem with that. This was another topic she and I had discussed at great length; and even though there was dialogue between us about a wedding, there was no great hurry. I was well aware of how important the desire to be a medical technologist was to her, and I wasn't going to even suggest that she give up her goal. Besides, there was much financial preparation to be done. I was nearing the end of my military obligation and would again be a civilian. This meant that I would have to find gainful employment and start a "nest egg" in which to have the funds needed to start a life together.

Yes, it took planning. And planned we did, with much enthusiasm on her part.

I bought for her what was known at the time as a "hope chest"; a redwood cedar chest in which to start accumulating household items. This was a common practice among young women at the time anticipating marriage. She also picked out a "pattern" of fine silverware, and I made sure that a complete place setting was added every Christmas and birthday. She started collecting cookware, linens, china; all the things that were necessary in which to start a home. I had no way of knowing at the time that I would not be the one sharing them with her. She finished her schooling and started her occupation as a medical technologist working for Crozer Hospital in Chester. The hospital had now dropped the other titles, and had expanded in construction, but it was in effect the same hospital that Judy and I were born in. I returned "to the states" from my tour of duty overseas on the island of Newfoundland in August, 1960. Our base there was home for one of the Air Refueling Wings within SAC. The duty of the huge KC-135 tankers based there, should war with the Soviet Union become a reality, would be to rendezvous with the bombers over the Atlantic to ensure that they were "topped-off" with fuel before entering Soviet airspace.

I landed at McGuire A.F.B on August 5ᵗʰ, Dad's birthday, and was discharged the same day; becoming a civilian once again. Everyone was surprised to see me so soon; and more surprised that I had been discharged. The Air Force had passed a regulation that those returning from overseas bases with less than a years service remaining on their enlistment had to either reenlist or "muster out" and be discharged. I had a little over eleven months remaining to my obligation and chose to reenter civilian life.

Since I was still only twenty years old and not yet legally able to rent an apartment, I reluctantly returned to "Mad" Avenue to live. The difference was that I had my own selfish interest in mind. I was going to use "home" as a "base of operations" while planning and preparing for a wedding—mine! It should again be established that in this point in time I still did not know that Judy and I were adopted! It would be almost another three years before I would have that fact revealed to me.

"Dad" was all but indifferent to my return. I had hardly unpacked before he informed me how much my room and board would be, and that he expected me to start looking for work immediately. I was neither surprised nor offended. I knew that I didn't want to stay there any longer than necessary, and the realization that I only had five and a half months until my twenty-first birthday was my incentive to "get things moving" as soon as possible.

On the other hand, Agnes seemed truly glad to see me. There was an undercurrent sense of loneliness about her. Her daughter, Joan, was in Hawaii; and Judy, at eighteen, had run off with "Buddy" to Elkton, Maryland and got

143

married; in defiance of Bill Ling's wishes. They were now living in their apartment in Norwood.

So, Agnes and I, for the first time, really started to get to know each other. I guess it was to be somewhat expected and reasonable, for now I was the only one home in whom to interact with.

I had saved the bulk of my service pay while stationed in Newfoundland and now had enough to purchase a car, a '58 Chevy Impala convertible; and I would take it upon myself to provide Agnes with transportation whenever possible. We would go to the food market together, and up to the train station when she went to work. She was now working part time for Speare Bros. in Chester, in the Women's Department. She had been a "buyer" for that department when she met Bill, with many trips to New York City on business. Her position now was much less glamorous, as that responsibility had long ago been filled by another.

Frequently, Dad and she left for work at the same time, but he refused to take her to the station. I was somewhat surprised at this given her condition with the diabetes. And no one in the family had any idea to what extent it was taking its toll. Her blood sugar always seemed to be "on the edge", and she was known to carry a package of hard candy known as "Charms" in her pocketbook, in case she had an episode that bordered on going into diabetic shock. "She could walk", was his attitude; and I once heard him verbally express it that way. The station was only five blocks away but he considered it "out of his way." It was during these excursions in the car that she and I would get to know, and understand, each other better.

Initially, I had a very difficult time finding employment. The country was still slowly recovering from a recession and there were not many good jobs available. That, plus the fact that I was only twenty years old without any knowledge of a

144

really usable trade made my search all the more frustrating. All I had to offer at this point was my know- ledge of teletype communications. For the exception of Western Union, or one of the airlines at the airport, there was not much in the offing in the way of employment. It was after many visits to the employment offices of the area's many corporations that I learned from Margie's father the American Viscose Corporation in Marcus Hook was looking for a technician for their quality control laboratory. He was employed there and knew some of the people in administration and had asked if there were any positions open. I was more than a little apprehensive about applying for the job. I had not even as much as taken high school chemistry, and I was certain that I would not qualify for the assignment. I was wrong. I was offered the position of "Lab Technician Trainee" three days after my interview. It was explained to me that the strong point in my favor in their decision to hire me was the fact my military obligation was completed. They could afford to take the chance to train me, and if things worked out they wouldn't lose me to the draft.

The company that I was working for was in the busi- ness of cellophane production. I would begin my training in basic laboratory techniques to be applied to the quality specs required to ensure a good product. These tasks would include both chemical and physical testing with duties such as performing titrations and tensile strengths.

The only immediate drawback to this job was that it required shift work. Producing a product is a 24 hour opera- tion, necessary for quotas to be met and schedules to keep. I had much experience with shift work; communications in the military never shut down. Still, I wasn't sure that it was something I wanted to continue to do for what might be my lifelong work history.

One of the first supervisors I worked for was a man named Bill Schermerhorn. When I was first introduced to him he asked me if I was any relation "to a Bill Ling" who worked for the Congoleum tile manufacturer in Trainer, approximately 3 miles away. I replied, "Yes, he's my father." Mr. Schermerhorn responded, "How about that!" "I used to work with him, about twelve years." " I knew he had two daughters, he used to talk about them all the time; but I never knew he had a son."

Bill Ling had worked with this man for over ten years and never mentioned me. It hurt. But then again, it only confirmed to me what I had always suspected; that I wasn't much more to my "father" than a tax deduction.

Margie and I spent most of our free time together, especially now that my job required me to work rotating shifts. This allowed me only one full weekend off per month, and when I had to work the second shift (3-11pm), and the "graveyard" shift (11pm -7am), we didn't see each other at all. I would find out much, much, later that this worked out fine for her but not for me. There was something else going on that I didn't know anything about.

On one of many dates to the Warner theatre in Wilmington, I became curious about the very large buildings that were directly across the street. After inquiring as to what they were, I learned that it was the corporate offices of the DuPont Company, the "giant" of the chemical industry. I surmised that they must have lab technicians employed some- where in the area and decided that I might try applying there for a job.

I visited the employment office there at the very first opportunity. I was subsequently informed that I was at the wrong location to be applying for such a position and was instructed to visit their research center just outside Wilmington proper, known as "The Experimental Station". I was to find out very shortly that, not only was this their main research site, it was also the largest industrial research facility in the world at the time. It was also the place where two of the Company's discoveries would become "household names." Both Nylon and Teflon were invented there.

After repeated visits to the employment office there, (I was persistent), I was finally granted an interview. Once again it would become apparent to me how choosing to get my military obligation out of the way upon graduation would work to my advantage.

It was now November of 1961, and in a few days they made me a job offer, and once again my draft status played a factor. I started two days before the Thanksgiving holiday break. It would now become my lifetime occupation, and I would work there for thirty-five years, retiring in 1996 at age 56. I should interject here that I was still living at "home"; in direct opposition to all my intentions of leaving on my twenty-first birthday, January 16th, 1961.

It was two days before, when I found Agnes sitting at the kitchen table crying. After asking her what was the matter (I thought she was ill), she literally begged me not to leave. She said, "Gene, please don't leave me here alone with Bill." She knew that I was about to move out. She had probably noticed the empty drawers to my dresser when she put the laundry away; for I had already started packing.

I truly felt sorry for her, she was caught in a situation that she was totally unhappy with, in effect a prisoner with no way out. After we talked for awhile, I relented and agreed that I would "tough it out" until Margie and I were married. I really didn't want to do this, but I was really moved by how distraught she was. Agnes was no actress, and I knew what she was feeling was genuine.

After starting with Dupont, something seemed to change in Margie's demeanor; or at least I perceived it as much.

There was a fluctuation in her moods and I couldn't decipher what was going on. It was very noticeable, and after pressing her about it, she assured me that there was nothing wrong; and in time she did seem to "snap out of it."

We continued to plan our wedding, visiting churches to see in which one we might be married. Neither of us were Christians and I guess it was simply a matter of picking a church which would be "a nice one" for the wedding ceremony. If it suited our interests we were both willing to become members if necessary.

We continued to talk and plan. And now with her education completed and her job at the hospital on track, we decided it was time to make our engagement official.

Both her parents gave us their blessing. And although there was not yet a truly "official announcement", the news quickly circulated among her family. Most had anticipated our relationship to move in that direction and there was much excitement and joy among all her relatives at the news. It was now July, 1963.

She asked me if we could go together to pick out her ring. I could see no reason why not to, and so I agreed. We started shopping for that all important purchase early in July, but it wasn't until Friday, July 26th that we left her house for the jewelry store in Chester to finally select _the_ engagement ring. She seemed unusually quiet, and it was then that she said to me, "Pull over, I have something I need to tell you." "What? What's the matter?" I asked. A short pause, and then she said, "I don't know how to tell you this, other than to just come out and say it." Then there was a longer pause. "I can't do this" she said, "I've been seeing someone else."

She obviously had been struggling about a decision to be made over the two relation- ships she had established; and now had taken that decision down to the wire. The reason for her mood swings was now apparent.

Devastated!! No other word for it! My mind was in a state of shock, confusion; all manner of incoherent thoughts scrambling through my brain, trying to make any sense to what I had just heard. After six years of involvement, and planning what I thought would be our wedding; she was breaking up with me. I was being dumped!

I learned later that her new "significant other" was one of her co-workers at the hospital. She would discreetly meet him there so as to keep her involvement with him a secret. This mutual friend of ours also revealed to me her new boyfriend never came to her house until after she had terminated our relationship. How she managed to manipulate everything in order to keep from being found out remains a mystery.

She apparently had been seeing this other person on and off since the days of my employment with American Viscose. I was totally unaware, and so were her parents. Knowing them, I was absolutely certain they would not have tolerated Margie "stringing me along" the way she did. They were 'straight up', honest people, and would not have allowed it. Had they known, I honestly believe they would have told me themselves.

The next day I shared with Agnes and Bill what had transpired the night before. It had been obvious to them that something was wrong, although they wouldn't pry. My eyes were red and I was finding it difficult to speak with any measure of composure.

After I told them there would be no wedding; that Margie had broken up with me the previous night, there was nothing but silence. Then after a few minutes they both expressed their sorrow for me, both of them were glassy-eyed, and then it was never mentioned again.

Agnes and Bill had been focused on something entirely different, that last week of July when Margie had terminated our "engagement." They had been planning and preparing for their annual two weeks of vacation down at the cottage in early August. I can remember that it was always taken during this period because we celebrated "dad's" birthday there every year.

All the employees at the Congoleum plant were expected to take their vacation at this time, the first full two weeks of that month; the exception being some key management personnel and a select crew of the craftsmen. The plant was shut down for those two weeks to permit the retooling of the machinery, and testing the compatibility of the use of new dyes for the flooring patterns. This was necessary to prepare the plant for the introduction of a new product line of flooring, traditionally introduced to the buying public every Fall.

Agnes's sister, our Aunt Anna, was now living with us on "Mad" Avenue. Bill had a small apartment for her added onto the Ridley Park end of the house after the death of her husband Samuel. She paid for the construction, and there was a small door in what used to be Judy and Joan's bedroom that gave access to her living quarters. She was a frail woman and needed to be checked on from time to time. She had been some measure of comfort for Agnes, but she didn't at all like Bill. In any case, she also would be going to Maryland on vacation with them.

On Saturday, morning August 3rd, they left for the beach and I said my goodbye's to them. I was looking at Agnes when I said, "Have a good time!" It would be the last thing I would ever say to her.

Agnes Currier McFerren Ling passed away of a massive heart attack at the family's cottage at Crystal Beach on August 5th, 1963. She was 53......... It was dad's birthday.

I never did find out the actual time given for Agnes's death but it must have been early. I received a phone call from Mom-mom that morning before leaving for my drive down to Wilmington and my job at "the station." Dad must have called home from the pay phone at the concession stand on the beach. Other than Mr. Shultz's phone at his store there, it was the only phone service available. Telephone service to any of the many cottages was not provided at the time.

Mom-mom's voice quivered as she broke the news but I don't recall what my immediate reaction was. I know that later I was dumbfounded, sad, and subdued; but most of all I felt guilty. Guilty because I had spoke to her just two days before and encouraged her "to have a good time", and now she was gone.

Also, I seemed to be in a state of confusion, as if it was all so surreal. My brain did not seem to want to process the information and deal with the event. I did not cry; I could not cry. But that would all catch up with me later.

Joan, no doubt, was devastated by the sudden death of her mother. Understandably, she took the news very hard, and the next few days were going to be very difficult for her. She and her family were now living in New Jersey, her husband being assigned to McGuire A.F.B.

Everyone in the family seemed to be in tears, except me. Even to this day I don't really understand why, unless for some reason my subconscious mind somehow would not let me deal with my emotions.

A few days later, at the viewing, "Dad" noticed that I was in what amounted to be "in denial" of what happened. He came over to me and said, "Gene, its ok, let it out." But I could not. It wasn't until the funeral itself that my emotions caught up with me.

151

Agnes was to be buried in Lawncroft Cemetery in Linwood; and I had agreed to be one of the pallbearers at Bill Ling's request. It turned out to be more emotionally difficult than I thought it might be.

Actually holding onto her casket proved to be traumatic; it brought to light the reality of the finality of her departure from this life. I broke down and cried and trembled almost uncontrollably. Even though we were not what one would call as being "close", there was an overwhelming sense of loss to me.

In addition to this; a little "footnote."

It would be almost forty years later before I would find out something astonishing about that day.

As I assisted in helping place her casket on the webbing that would lower Agnes to her final resting place, little did I know that our birth mother, Dora Killen Brinton Hall, was buried just a little over one-hundred feet behind me.

I would not have this knowledge until 38 years later, May 21st, 2001.

Everyone in the family seemed to be in some sort of limbo, a kind of foggy oblivion, for a time after Agnes's death. I guess none of us truly realized what an impact her pass- ing would have on us all. And not everyone had someone in whom to find emotional support in dealing with the loss. Judy had "Buddy", Joan had Jack, and Bill Ling had his mother, Mom-mom, in which to confide in and find solace. Anna and I, however, had no one in which to find comfort and support; at least not initially.

It seemed that it was now Anna's turn to ask me not to leave her alone in the house with Bill; which she did shortly after the funeral. She didn't want to be alone, period! She implored me to spend some time visiting her in her small apartment. We really didn't know each other that well at this point, most of her interaction with the household had been with the women. Often times, she would be the "fourth" for the card games of pinochle that I have mentioned earlier in my story. She, Agnes, Judy, and Joan, always seemed to have a great time around the kitchen table playing the game, both there at home, and down at the cottage.

I honored her request not to leave. I would take the time, perhaps two times a week, to spend some time with her, if for only an hour or so. I would knock on the access door from the bedroom that was Judy's and Joan's and she would let me in. Invariably, she would offer me tea or a soft drink, and then we would talk. Others in the family, Judy and Joan specifically, couldn't understand this new relationship between "Aunt Anna" and me. Unwittingly, I think we became each others support, and in our own simplistic way, without realizing it, we found the comfort we needed in dealing with the loss of Agnes in each other. One thing was for sure, neither of us was going to get any support from Bill Ling, he never spoke to either of us about this tragic loss we shared in.

It was on one of these visits with her that I learned of Judy and my adoption. It came out, unintentionally, in her story relayed to me regarding Agnes's response to Bill's disclosure to her about it; and she, Anna, had momentarily forgotten her promise.

It was a slip of the tongue on Anna's part. She had no sooner mentioned the word adoption that she covered her mouth with her hand. Since "the cat was out of the bag", she continued to say that Agnes had made her promise that she would not tell me or Judy; but now that Agnes was gone, she no longer felt bound to that pact. And so there it was; the officer who interviewed me while I was in basic training had it right, and I had it wrong; Judy and I had indeed been adopted. I often entertain the idea whether I might have been successful in obtaining additional information, at that time, if I had only given some credibility to what I was being told during that security interview; what difference it may have made in how things would have played out.

But, hindsight seems always to be 20/20, and Judy and I will never know.

For awhile, it was no problem continuing to live in Dad's house, we rarely saw each other. Every weekday I would be up and out of the house and on my way to Delaware, and my job, before he got out of bed. In the evenings I would be out carousing around as an alternative to being "home", and most of the time he had already retired by the time I arrived. Sometimes he would be the one out "for the evening" and I would be the one home early. I would make sure I was in my room before he pulled in the driveway.

I did all I could do to avoid any complaint from him or confrontation. I continued to make sure the grass was cut, take out the trash, and I kept my room in order. I knew that it didn't take much to set him off. Everything was fine until mid October, and then we "had it out." And, I don't know what it is with the month of October but it seems that most of the major events in my life have transpired during that month.

I don't even clearly remember exactly what precipitated our argument. I know that he had arrived home earlier in the evening than usual, and was preparing dinner for himself in the kitchen. In retrospect, I think it may have been that I had made, for myself, a cup of hot tea and some toast, leaving the dishes in the sink. He stomped into the living room where I was seated reading the newspaper. He started screaming at me something to the effect that, "Just because Agnes is gone, I'm not your damn maid!" He continued to "rag on me", almost out of control. It was then that I threw down the paper, jumped up out of the chair, and face to face, I yelled back! "ENOUGH! I'm tired of you taking your damn frustrations out on me!"

He didn't give me time to continue my angry rebuttal. He quickly raised his arm, and with his hand pointing to the kitchen door said, "GET OUT"! That was it; that's all it took. I packed practically everything I owned into my '58 Impala, and left.

I had two dollars in my pocket, and two days to payday. I didn't know what I was going to do. But in a sense I was okay with it, I didn't want to be there anyhow.

I can clearly remember one other thing about this incident.

I was angry, and angry mostly at God! It seemed to me He was giving me a steady diet of setbacks, and again I perceived Him as being a celestial bully, just as I had done in my childhood. Nothing was going right in my life, and I blamed Him for the downturn.

I was livid! In fact, I claimed that there were no words in the English language that could adequately express my anger. I can clearly recall shaking my fist at the heavens, and screaming at the top of my voice; "Why do you hate me?" If anyone in the neighborhood could hear me, and perhaps someone had, they would have thought I was drunk, a babbling idiot, or both.

It was immediately after that little tirade when Pop-pop's seemingly prophetic remark returned to my memory; "Your life can fall apart very quickly, without any warning."

And it had.

When my heart was grieved and my spirit embittered,
I was senseless and ignorant; I was a brute beast before
you.

—Psalm 73: 21, 22 (NIV)

155

All those events that had just happened to me transpired within three months time. It was if I was being pushed under a sea of crisis after crisis, without given time to come up for air. I viewed the events that had just become part of my life's experience totally outside my control, with the possible exception of my angry response to my "father's" verbal abuse. My anger consumed me, turning my attitude towards life sour. Again, I deemed that I was not at all responsible for what had happened, those things that would now become part of my personal history.

But now, "I" was going to be in control, "I" was the one going to make the decisions; "I" was the one going to set the direction for my life! Unfortunately, the "direction" was the wrong one, and it was all because of my furious state of mind. My life would continue to take a nose-dive because of my foolish decisions, and I found myself spiraling down…..down….down.

I slept in my car with all my belongings for two nights. I used the craftsmen's shower room at work to shower and shave. I borrowed a few dollars from some of my closest co-workers to tide me over until payday, necessary in order to feed myself.

I had money, lots of it, my problem was that I couldn't get to it. My situation had happened at the worst of all possible times. My money, savings that was supposed to be used for a wedding, was tied-up in the Credit Union at "the station."

We had all been sent "fliers" in our mail notifying us it was going to be closed for two days in order to make a move to another building. I don't need to tell you what two days they would turn out to be!

When payday arrived I decided to stay at the "Y" for a few days to collect my thoughts, and started looking in the classifieds to find a permanent place to live that was within my means. I had actually contemplated staying at the city's "Sunday Breakfast Mission" on Front Street, a shelter for homeless men in the Wilmington area.

After learning that those staying there must leave each and every morning with all their belongings, I opted for the "Y." I just needed a place to stay for a few days to sort things out before committing myself to any kind of long term arrangement.

I would eventually return to 'the mission" after having retired from the Dupont Company; but not as a resident, but rather as a part time employee, having a token appreciation for the plight of the homeless.

I was totally unfamiliar with much of the Wilmington area, so I began to ask my co- workers about various apartment complexes, and if they had any recommendations.

It was then that I met a new chemist just hired with the company and newly assigned to our research group. He informed me of the boarding house he was living in over on 24th Street in the city. The owner, an elderly woman, was looking for another boarder. He gave me the phone number and I called right away, setting up an interview for later that afternoon. I moved in the next day.

There were now three boarders residing there, all males, and all "DuPont." She had explained to me during the interview she only rented her rooms to DuPont employees, for two reasons. First, it was well known that their jobs were secure, and therefore her income from the rooms was secure. There was a time when job security at DuPont was a "given." One only had to get past the first five-year probationary period to obtain what amounted to a life-time job. How times have changed.

The second reason was her opinion that DuPont employees were of a better character; she never had a problem collecting the rent from them, as she had from some other previous renters who were not from "The Company." So, if one was not "from DuPont" they simply were not going to reside there in her home.

It was very comfortable, an atypical four-bedroom house; with my own room. And after spending the previous several days living out of my car, and the "cubbyhole" of a room at the 'Y', I knew that this would suit me just fine, at least temporarily, and I was going to be "ok."

I could have, and probably should have, taken my savings from the credit union and purchased furniture and set up an apartment of my own. But I could not bring myself to do that. Even though it had been what the funds had been saved for, I couldn't emotionally handle it. After all, I reasoned, I was supposed to be doing that kind of shopping with a new wife by my side.

I decided I was going to enjoy the money; I was going to "splurge." I had angrily decided that <u>every dime</u> I spent was going to be on <u>me</u>, and not some "damn woman." Being in that frame of mind, I took "the wedding money" and bought myself a new car; a '64 Chevy Malibu Super-Sport, with wire-wheel spinners.

I was out every night; off to the taverns, Go-Go bars, and "honky-tonks", spending those "dimes", determined to have a good time. And, I told myself that I WAS having a good time, but in reality I knew that I was hurting deep within my spirit.

I lived carelessly, recklessly, and started drinking. I was no stranger to alcohol, any one who has been in the military has certainly been introduced to it. But now I didn't put any limits on myself. It got to a point where I would consume a six-pack of beer <u>before</u> I went out for my nightly excursions.

My anger, frustration, and hurt were leading me on a destructive course. I just didn't care about anything! Anything, other than my job. At least I had enough sense to make sure that I protected it. No matter how bad I felt the next morning after my near all-night escapades, I made sure I went to work. I knew that everything hinged on a job and an income.

To illustrate what my state of mind was during this low point in my life, I will now divulge something that was a nightly practice of mine for the longest time, and at the time of this writing I think it is known only by my wife.

I did not know many people in the Wilmington area when I first moved here. So it was not unusual for me to travel up to Pennsylvania and "hang-out" with my buddies from my school days at a tavern know as "The Haddon Inn", located on McDade Boulevard in Folcroft.

Every night I would take with me a stopwatch that was used in my job to gauge, and time, the drop-wise introduction of liquid chemical reactants into a reaction vessel.

When my evening was over, shooting pool and drinking beer, I would start the stopwatch as I left the "Haddon's" parking lot and "fly" back to Delaware. When I pulled up to the curb at my new "home", I would stop the watch and note the amount of time it took me to return. The next night, and every subsequent one, my goal was to beat the previous nights time! Every trip home was faster, and Faster, and FASTER than the night before.

It finally resulted in three accidents within one year, luckily none of them serious; as far as personal injury to me or anyone else. However, it was very hard on my Malibu, most of the year of 1964 in was in the shop for repairs. I had also been dropped by two insurance companies during that year and now I was appointed to another, as an assigned risk. My insurance premiums were now higher than my car payments, and my budget simply could not handle the cost. Because of my foolishness I would eventually have to sell my car, which I did in March of 1965; a direct result of the anger that had consumed me.

One other episode bears mentioning before I move away from this time in my life when I had bought my very first new car.

I had purchased my Malibu from King Chevrolet, in Chester, PA. in November of '63. It was early on a Saturday morning in January, when I drove up to the dealership for the first "new-car" checkup. I was hoping to be first in line, but indeed, someone else had arrived sooner. It was a Super-Sport just like mine, except for the color and no wire wheels. We were both early in our arrival and stayed in the warmth of our cars.

When the dealership finally opened for business, out stepped a young lady from the vehicle in front of me. It was Margie.

We were both noticeably surprised to see each other. We initially offered each other a token, 'Hi', and not much more; a very awkward situation to be sure. After a few seemingly long, excruciating moments, there was some small talk, centered around the most logical safe topic there was, our new cars.

Then we both noticed a mechanic approaching us obviously ready to start his day. Before he got to us to discuss the business at hand, she said to me; "When we're done here, do you want to go set some coffee?" I wasn't sure if I should, or even if I really wanted to; for I knew I wasn't over my anger. But, half curious, partly suspicious, and definitely cautious, I agreed.

We decided to meet up the street at "Linton's", a popular drive-in restaurant just four blocks away. On the way there, I told myself that our conversation would take place in her car; I wanted the option to leave whenever I wanted to.

The small talk continued, and I no longer remember what most of it was about. I do remember that she apologized and said, "I'm sorry for what I did." There was no response from me; I said nothing, not a word! We talked some more; I asked about her parents, informed her I had moved to Wilmington, and we shared a host of other little "tidbits" of information between us; long since forgotten. Neither her new boyfriend, nor whether or not I was seeing someone was mentioned by either of us.

Towards the end of our conversation, she said to me, "So, when are you coming to dinner?" I just looked at her, and again, said nothing. I could not determine if this was an attempt on her part to get back together, or if she was (and here's that term again) just "baiting me", to see what my response would be.

There is a saying that goes something like, "First time, shame on you! Second time, shame on me!"

She had six years of my life, and she had "played me", probably for the better part of the last two years; I wasn't prepared to give her any more.

It was now almost six months since she broke up with me, and I was still hurting. I had not gotten over her, I even admitted to myself that I was still in love with her; and I would continue to be so for some time to come, but I could no longer *trust* her. I was simply not going to spend the rest of my life with a woman that I couldn't trust; in no way was I going to put myself in a position where I would be constantly wondering if my life's partner was being faithful.

I got out of her car, wished her well, said "goodbye", closed her door, and walked to my Malibu.

I had essentially walked away from her.
It was the hardest thing I have ever done.

Each heart knows its own bitterness,....
—Proverbs 14:10 (NIV)

CHAPTER NINE

UPTURN

A FATHERLESS FATHER

My life in the year that was 1964 could best be described with the analogy of a pinball machine.

That was me.

A ball flying uncontrollably out of the chute, bouncing around from one thing to the next, with no real purpose or direction; not knowing where I was going, nor looking back to where I had been. All I was interested in was accumulating as many points as I could on the scoreboard of pleasure and experiences. I guess that I was trying to forget, or deny, the incredible hurt and loneliness that seemed to overwhelm me.

As it would turn out, there would be two distinct groups of people I would become involved with during the better part of that year.

The first group, were "old" friends, guys I had known from my school years, and some even from my childhood. The second group I would come to know by a new friendship established at the boarding house where I was now living.

Three of my buddies from "the Haddon" worked for the airlines at the "Philly" airport. One worked for Delta, and the other two for what used to be Eastern Airlines. The one for Delta worked in aircraft maintenance, and the other two were baggage handlers for the other airline. They were the support people one sees driving those little carts in tow, shuttling the luggage back and forth from the aircraft to the terminal.

One of the "perks" of their jobs was they all three got a free trip to anywhere in the continental United States once a year, dependent on space available. The only expense they were responsible for were the taxes applied to the tickets.

They were planning a trip to Miami Beach and invited me and another friend, whom I didn't know, to join them. The two of us had to pay regular fare, since neither of us were employed by the airlines.

The five of us left for Florida in early May for a ten day vacation. There we frequented the many go-go bars and nightclubs in our rented new 1964 Thunderbird.

Of course, a couple of trips to Miami's *Playboy Club* were imperative, access granted by a borrowed "key" from one of our friends so we could spend some time with the "bunnies". There were many other up-scale clubs, and some that were not, where we spent our money without keeping track of how much was passing through our fingers.

Then, a trip up to Ft. Lauderdale, and a flight over to Bimini Island on "Mackey Airlines", for a day of snorkeling.

And, when we weren't doing all those things, we would be on the beach checking out all the young ladies in their bikinis, or at the dog track; drinking beer and losing our money on the dogs we knew were "a sure bet!"

You get the idea, just doing the crazy things that young men in their twenty's do, seeking what they think is "the good life"; and after a time, realizing how empty it is. The enjoyment the pleasure gives is only temporary; and essentially, meaningless!

And, the book of Ecclesiastes, in The Holy Scriptures, has much to say on the subject of "meaningless!"

Now, for the second group.

One of the residents that shared the boarding house with me was one Elmer Durfey. When we first met each other, it was evident that we had at least two things in common, DuPont and Wyoming.

He was born and raised there, his home being in Greybull, located almost in the center of the state near the Montana border. And, I, of course, had been stationed at the airbase located near Cheyenne.

We would talk about "Frontier Days", the Wyoming State Fair, held every August just outside that city. He said his family attended the fair every year, and after discussing the particular fair held in 1957, it was apparent that we both were there at the same time. It was also obvious that he and I shared a common interest in the history of the Old West.

We soon became friends, and in time discussed the idea of venturing away from the boarding house and jointly renting an apartment. We knew that both of our DuPont jobs were stable, and there should be no problem in sharing the costs. So we found an apartment across town on a street named Park Place; and NO, it didn't have anything to do with the game of Monopoly! It was a good move, each of us were now closer to our place of employment, and Elmer would often walk to work.

He worked for the Finance Department in the corporate offices downtown, and I, once again, was a research lab technician at The Experimental Station only about a mile away.

It seemed that just about every Friday he would be off to catch an early evening train to New York City for the weekend. Naturally, after awhile I became curious, so I asked him, "What's up with going to New York City every weekend?" He explained that he had an old college friend who was now in the Army and stationed there, helping process new recruits at a facility known as "Whitehall."

Since there were no military accommodations available in the city, they were authorized "separate rations" and billeted in civilian quarters. His friend, Randy, shared an apartment with three other recruiters in Queens, at the expense of the government.

The apartment just next door to them was shared by four girls, all airlines reservationists. These eight people became good friends, none of them romantically involved with each other, and dubbed themselves "the clan"; and they seemed to go everywhere around the city together.

At first I wasn't sure about the name "clan", with its implication pointing towards the 'KKK'; but then I was to learn of the one who coined the phrase. He was one of Elmer's friend's roommates. He went by the name of "James", but his real name was Jamie McPherson, and he was obviously of a very strong Scottish heritage.

On one of his visits Elmer mentioned me in response to their questions as to where he was living in Wilmington, and not long after that I was invited by the group to accompany Elmer up to the city for a visit.

The thing can I remember about my first trip up to visit "the clan" was that Elmer and I had no sooner arrived when we were informed that we were all going to a party "across town." When we inquired as to who was giving the party, their response was, "we don't know, we just heard about it two hours ago, from one of the girls next door!" It was considered an "open party", a strange phenomenon for the times. One only had to be aware of the event, be of legal age (since there was always alcohol involved), and the only requirement for those who wanted to participate was they were expected to contribute to the festivity. So, we would readily visit a "deli" and a liquor store close by to the apartment complex in which to purchase our "tickets" to these events; and then we would be off to the subway station.

There was also an unwritten understanding amongst us that we would stay together whenever we did our traveling to these gatherings. That was an ironclad agreement between us, the only exception being when we would be staying close by the apartments or traveling "uptown" to center city.

We always went as a group and left as a group, the ten of us, and we never split up; the old adage of safety in numbers applied. Our new friends knew which sections of the city one simply did not travel into at night. Our transportation always entailed using the subway system, and although there were areas of the city that were perfectly safe to travel during the daytime, these same places were very foolish to venture into after the sun went down.

We never had any question of safety in traveling anywhere we wanted to go, or at any of the parties we went to. These gatherings were unquestionably some of the best I have ever attended, and certainly the most interesting.

New York City has been described as "the great melting pot', and in a real way these gatherings could have been labeled the same. All of them had a truly diverse representation of people attending; ages of people in their twenties, up to some elderly in their seventies. Usually, it typically numbered about thirty participants; from all types of social , ethnic, racial, and intellectual backgrounds; a true mix of people. There was always plenty of refreshments, conversation, dancing, and of course, booze. There were some very well educated people, and others that didn't seem to be able to express their thoughts in a complete sentence. Some of the conversation could become somewhat heated, but seldom was there a truly belligerent argument , and never an altercation. I enjoyed going to them, and there would be many.

My first trip up to the city with Elmer was a grand time. I was very well received by "the clan", and I was invited to come back anytime. I started going up to visit every other weekend.

I continued to drink heavily, and I am now well aware of the unquestionable protection of the Lord through all those foolish years. It has become evident that alcoholism was rampant within my biological family's history, something that I have only found out about in recent years. And, since it has been well establish that the propensity toward that disease is heredity, I can see how the Lord, in His sovereignty, changed the events in my life that would redirect me from the road I was traveling down.

In the meantime, however, I continued to drink. We all did. Every activity, every occasion, seemed to include alcohol to some extent. Even when we were at the Worlds Fair, which New York City hosted in 1964, we found ourselves spending more than our fair share of time at the Rheingold and Schaefer exhibits.

Usually the girls in our group, in addition to the guys, always had a continual array of drink available, and between the two apartments, there was a seemingly endless supply of booze that was never depleted.

At first, I wondered if this practice was only indicative of this particular group I had become involved with, for, even back in Wilmington, I wouldn't say that every function involved the use of alcohol. Later, it became obvious this was just what seemed to be part of the "New Yorker's" culture. It appeared that no one in the city could do without their highball, martini, or beer. It was probably fortunate I didn't live there; with the accepted protocol of one being constantly seen with a drink in hand, and no one giving it a second thought. I might have found myself well on the way to becoming a true alcoholic, had I been habitually part of that social order.

One of the persons from the group was a girl named Cindy. She started to show an interest in me during my second visit, dropping little hints about going out "just for a cup of coffee" together. I told her (with what I recall was a very hard look), "I'm not at all interested." The words no sooner left my mouth than I regretted saying them. I could see by the unmistakable momentary look of rejection and hurt on her face that I had offended her, and that wasn't like me; I was not in the practice of knowingly hurting people.

I called her aside and explained my situation; the fact I was recovering from a failed relationship and not to take it personal, that I was still angry with women in general; and I guess it showed. My bitterness and hurt during that time wouldn't let me entertain any level of a relationship with a member of the fairer sex. Still, I knew that in the back of my mind I craved the company and companionship of a woman, but I refused to allow myself to acknowledge it. I was very stubborn back then; and in some ways, I still am.

It was now mid-June, and I had not brought myself back to the dating scene; I was still spending those "dimes" on myself. But it would turn out to be Cindy who would slowly chisel down the barrier I had put in place. At the time, I was focused primarily on myself, and I thought that I was the only one who could hurt that bad.

I was wrong.

During our conversations in subsequent weeks, I would find out that she, Cindy, was also trying to retrieve her emotions from a relationship that suddenly disintegrated. The two of us now had something we could identify with, a kind of empathy towards each other over the hurt we were both experiencing. Unintentionally, at first, we started to cautiously confide in each other, becoming somewhat of each other's mentor. We were practically strangers, true, but I think we found a level of safety in that fact; we could be very open and objective in our comments and thoughts; trying to help each other figure out "what happened?" to our individual relationships. It turned out to be very therapeutic for both of us; she and I had developed our own micro support group, and we became good friends.

At some point, I had asked her, with a grin, if she wanted to "go get that cup of coffee" she had mentioned about at an earlier time. With a grin that surpassed mine, she said "Yeah, sure!" Then we both smiled and kind of chuckled to ourselves, and each other.

We would periodically excuse ourselves from the group to visit a coffee house nearby the apartments to have our discussions. Sometimes we would leave the group to take in a movie, or spend a few hours in a small tavern. I guess one could classify these as "dates", and our friends in "the clan" saw it that way. We, however, considered it just an opportunity to exchange our thoughts with some measure of privacy. There wasn't any real romantic interest for either of us, we were both still very much "gun-shy", extremely cautious; and we had established from the beginning that our relationship was to be limited to "just friends."

It is my conviction that nothing occurs by happenstance, and it is my personal belief this encounter of Cindy's and mine was no accident. I have come to realize the Lord's providential hand in directing the two of us together. The

Lord understood the magnitude of the personal and pro-found pain that she and I were <u>both</u> experiencing, and our involvement with each other was no chance meeting. There is no doubt in my mind that we both benefited from our talks, giving each other the support and understanding that we both so desperately needed, and I know for a fact that these talks helped me in the healing process.

I don't clearly recall when Elmer and I completely cur-tailed our trips up to New York, but I know it was shortly after that Summer, and most likely sometime in early Sep-tember. Elmer was now dating a co-worker from his office on a somewhat regular basis and his trips became sporadic. My trips also became less and less, mainly because I didn't have the extra finances. The repair costs to my car were taking up whatever extra money I had, and the funds for these ventures up to "The City" were just not there. Also, I was to learn from Elmer, when he returned from one of his solo trips, that Cindy had left New York, and her job, and moved back to her hometown outside Ithaca. She made Elmer promise her that he would pass on a message to me. She said, the best I can recall, "She valued our time together, our talks helped her a lot; that I was a good friend and she wished me well."

And, for me, without getting the chance to tell her, I felt the same way.

So, the trips for me were now history, a phase in my life that had come and gone, and I never again returned to "the clan." But even after all these years, I still have some very fond memories of those times.

There are two other things I can clearly recall during that September of 1964.

One was on a Tuesday evening after returning to our apartment from our usual food shopping at the local A&P every other week. Elmer was in the process of cooking his

171

very thick T-bone steak with onions and potatoes in an oversized iron "skillet", as they referred to a frying pan out West. And one of his idiosyncrasies was he liked to sing while he cooked! So, there he was, merrily cooking his dinner with a cooking fork in one hand and a beer in the other, singing to his heart's content! I was always glad when he was finished preparing his meals.

I was in the living room watching the nightly news, with President Johnson once again telling the country, and the world, "we seek no wider war." I got ever so tired of hearing that phrase during the era that was the Vietnam conflict.

Then there was a knock on our door.

I answered the door with my trusty can of Schaefer brew in hand, to be met by three nicely dressed men in coat and tie, and I immediately noticed that all three had Bibles in hand. Without thinking, my initial response went something like, "Uh-Oh, here we go again."

They introduced themselves, and explained they were from the First Baptist Church "just up the street" (actually about a half-mile away) on Pennsylvania Avenue. They were visiting around the neighborhood and inviting people who didn't have a church to visit theirs.

Before I could excuse ourselves by explaining that we were just getting ready to eat, Elmer spoke up and said, "let them in!" Elmer liked discussing "religion", he was of the Christian Scientist persuasion, a "faith" that I have never understood, and attended the church which was truly "just up the street", less than half a block away. He attended regularly, and I didn't attend church at all. He had invited me to join him several times, but once again, I wasn't into "religion."

I was very uncomfortable that these gentlemen were there in our apartment, and I didn't know why. I guess it may have been that in the back of my mind I knew that God would not have approved of the way I was living. I was very much "in the world", with both feet firmly planted in it. I was still angry with God, and totally rebellious.

How deep we were, Elmer and I, in pursuing "worldly pleasure" was evident by the way our apartment was decorated.

I could almost hear the gasps of the three when they came in, and I still think one of them muttered something to the effect of, "Oh, my!"

Our walls were "decorated" with probably no less than a dozen Playboy centerfolds. I don't know who was more ill at ease, Elmer and me, or them. I did notice, however, that the youngest of the three, about my age, was struggling to keep his eyes from wandering to the walls, to "sneak a peak", as it were. I found it somewhat amusing, but also comforting, that even Christians could be healthy young men, with hormones bouncing "all around the place."

They wouldn't take Elmer's bait to enter into a lengthy discussion of the differences in the various denominations. They were graciously respecting his views, but steered clear of any real debate. As I recall, they never did really get the opportunity to share the gospel, and after about a twenty minute visit, they left; but not before again inviting us to their church.

I don't remember Elmer and me discussing the visit, or if we did, it was very brief. I do remember thinking about the evening, and one of my thoughts was, "He, (God) doesn't give up, does He!? I would find out in the future, that........ No, He does not!

Another thing that was starting for change for me was my attitude on the subject of dating. Aside from the "dates" that Cindy and I were engaged in, I had not been out with another girl since Margie broke off our relationship the previous July. I slowly began backing off from my hardnosed stance and started dating once more; but I had made some ground rules, for I was determined not to even get remotely seriously involved with anyone.

There were only three rules, and they were relatively simple. First, I would ask a prospective date out only once; either she wanted to go out with me, or she didn't. Secondly, there would never be more than two dates with any one particular girl, period! And thirdly, it had to be my idea. We were entering a stage in American culture where it was beginning to be commonplace for a girl to initiate a date. There were more than a few times when a girl had asked me, "So, when are you and I going to go out?" I shied away from all such proposals. I was from the "old school", and still considered it forward for a girl to make such a move. Typically, my response would be something to the effect of, "I don't remember me asking you, do you?" That would usually be the end of the matter.

The two-dates-only limit was incorporated as a "safety valve", it prevented me from developing any real interest in pursuing any kind of a relationship. Of course, there <u>were</u> instances in which I was very much tempted in to pursuing a third date, but then I would remind myself, reviewing the policies I had made, and then stubbornly heeded that "flashing red light." It was a warning and a wake up call; but most of all it was a defensive mechanism. I still had maintained a near total distrust of women; there was no way I was going to "get involved" and once again become vulnerable. Besides, there was no point in it. After all, I had every intention of remaining a bachelor, and promised myself that I would never again put myself in a position where there was even a remote chance of being hurt the way I had been; of going through the long and difficult process of handling the rejection, pain, and the almost complete destruction of one's self-esteem. I was determined to "play it safe." Never again would I allow myself to become completely emotionally involved with another woman.

Ah! Never say never!

The next thing I had to consider about my future was where I was going to live. I surmised that if I was going to pursue the bachelor lifestyle, I might as well get on with it as soon as possible. This would entail going off on my own and set up an apartment for myself. I discussed this with Elmer, mainly to inform him of my intentions so that he could pursue looking for another roommate. I moved during the third week of October, almost a year to the very day my "father" had thrown me out.

My new home was to be an apartment over on 24th street that was small but very comfortable. It was clean, cozy, and located in a very safe section of the city, and the cost for the rent worked very nicely into my budget.

Another decision I made before my move was that my new apartment would be decorated differently. I rationalized that I wasn't going to eventually become a middle-aged man with "centerfolds" on my walls. Although my thinking, and planning, was geared to the distant future, I decided now was the time to get started. After all, I had resigned myself to the fact that I would remain single; so, I reasoned, why shouldn't I start developing my "bachelor pad" right away?

The apartment would portray a more neutral theme, probably something based on nature, a favorite subject of mine, and would be much more tasteful. Even though I didn't have the funds to make it "elegant", in any sense of the word, at least it would appear somewhat mature.

Elmer's decision was to stay put, taking up the financial slack that I had created after I moved out. He began to like living by himself, and I did also. However, we still continued an active friendship, carousing around together several nights a week; along with Dave and Tom, two roommates who lived in an apartment over ours on Park Place.

The four of us could be found at any number of the taverns and nightspots in downtown Wilmington on a weekday evening, except Fridays. Those two nights were consistently set aside for the two dances, held on alternating weeks, known as, "The Free Radicals", and "Bobalu."

Both of theses singles dances were the brain-child of three lab technicians that worked at "the station." One of my co-workers, Lou Lardear, was the only one of the three that I knew, the other two worked for a different department of the company at the site, but I never met them, and I only knew of their first names, Al and Bob.

"Free radicals", is a chemical term, and they thought it novel to name one of the dances as such; referring to the singles as "free", the other half of the description of those attending as "radical." That particular dance was held at the Manor Lion's Club in Wilmington Manor, off the DuPont Highway just South of Wilmington, and of course, always on a Friday night.

Alternating with that particular event, and night, was the "Bobalu" dance, which was held at the Fournier Hall in the predominately Italian section of Wilmington.

The original name was formed from the three who organized and promoted it; Bob, Al, and Lou. The initial title of the dance was distinctly pronounced as "Bob-Al-Lou", but rapidly developed, or deteriorated, by those who regularly attended to "Bobalu."

These two social gatherings became very popular with the young adults from the area, and they were always well attended. They normally started in mid-September and continued until Memorial Day. I'm sure that anyone who was a young single person during that period, and lived in the Wilmington area, has very fond memories of them.

Elmer, Dave, Tom, and myself, went to just about all of them, at least at first. That was going to change about the time March, 1965 rolled around.

I found myself slowly drifting into a truly solitary lifestyle. It was towards the end of March, approaching April 1st, April fool's day, and I no longer had a car. Indeed, because of my foolish behavior I now found myself grounded; I was paying dearly for those "nights of the stopwatch."

What used to be a very active and prolific social life was now literally "curbed." I now had to depend on others for transportation to and from events, and was limited to whatever their social interests were, and they weren't always mine. The only exception was once a month I would make it a point to rent a car for the weekend, a treat that I relished and would not deny myself.

That particular weekend was always very, very, well planned. Any department store shopping I needed to do was done then. A trip up to Pennsylvania to see some of my friends was usually incorporated, but for certain, one of the most important events included a date. I would commit myself to the car rental centered solely on those plans.

And, it seemed to be enough for me; I got comfortable with my situation, and the idea of being able to splurge once a month gave me something to look forward to. Also, it made me plan very carefully in order to utilize the time to my best advantage. Plus the very fact that the other weekends were essentially "uneventful" permitted me to have the funds for the car rental. This new lifestyle would suit me very well, at least for awhile. Even the "once-a-month" date was acceptable; I mean, after all, I wasn't going to get involved with anyone for the long-term anyhow, right?!

The Summer of 1965 was a surprise. It turned out to be a lot better than I had anticipated. Probably because the four of us guys continued to socialize together most weekends.

Doing things like trips to Gettysburg, Washington D.C., Rehobeth Beach here in Delaware, and if not there, some of the many beaches on the "Jersey Shore."

I still, however, continued with my own solo sabbatical excursions once a month, not bothering to offer transportation for the trips with the other guys. They seemed to appreciate the fact that I needed a "my weekend" to myself, doing the things I needed to do and seeing the people I needed to see. And since we all contributed to the cost of transportation during our other journeys I felt comfortable in not offering to provide 'the ride' the one weekend per month that I had a car.

On the weekend that I had the car in July, I decided to find a 'quiet' location at one of the beaches in New Jersey, as opposed to the partying atmosphere found at most of the vacation spots. I drove over to Barnegat Bay and found a secluded section on the beach, put down my blanket, turned on my radio, took out a 'Pepsi' from the cooler and proceeded to read my "Black Belt" magazine. I was practicing Judo at this stage of my life and that particular magazine was, at the time, about the only martial arts publication available.

For about forty minutes there was nobody around. I had practically the whole beach to myself with no more than ten people in sight. I was positioned about eighty yards from the shoreline and the other beachgoers where further away from me than that.

I opened my soda, then read my material until I was finished with the liquid refreshment that was helping me keep cool. When I was finished, I laid down and placed the radio next to my head. It was very peaceful and I was thoroughly enjoying the solitude; a solitude about to be interrupted.

About fifteen minutes after I had gotten peacefully settled in, I detected the unmistakable sound of footprints walking close by my blanket in the sand. I didn't bother to look up, I just listened to the sound slowly fade away from my hearing. I didn't really care who it was as long as they continued to move on away from me.

An undeterminable amount of time passed before I felt the need to cool myself off in the ocean. I sat up and briefly allowed my eyes adjust to the effects the bright sun had on them before heading to the shoreline. It was then that I saw her.

The person who previously walked past me was a very, very attractive long- haired brunette, about my age, wearing a two piece white bathing suit that accentuated the nice tan she was obviously working on. She had positioned her blanket only twenty yards away from me. Most guys would have been thrilled to death; but I found myself irritated.

I took a few seconds to look around and noticed that the beach was still practically deserted. I can remember thinking to myself, "Damn, she's got the whole damn beach to choose a place and she has to sit here."

While I was thinking all of this, she was sitting facing me, applying the lotion that would contribute to her tan. She was looking at me and gave me a nice smile. It wouldn't last though, for I took a moment to prepare, and return, the most emphatic scowl that I could muster!

I can clearly recall my thinking; "Pull in your claws, woman! You're baiting me and and it's not going to work!" Her smile immediately faded and she then turned away from me an continued her application of lotion.

I then got up and strolled down to the waters edge making sure I didn't look in her direction. I held a conversation with myself on the way, thinking; "Yeah, that's what it is, baiting. And, just like a fisherman, they bait, catch, and release! They use all kinds of lures to 'catch a guy', and then after they tire of him, throw him back; just like Margie did! No, thanks; I gave that girl my heart and she threw it back; I'm keeping it!" I remember this solitary conversation very well; it epitomized my frame of mind at the time, for I was still licking my wounds over that broken relationship, and still angry.

I cooled myself off in the ocean waves for about ten minutes. When I returned to my blanket the pretty girl was gone. I lay back down, repositioned my radio, and settled in for a nap. The last thing I can remember before drifting off was congratulating myself for adhering to the rules I had made. I was the one who would be initiating any kind of a relationship, not them.

Almost all of the girls I went out with at the time were from what I had termed "the pool at work." They were the secretaries and mail girls I interacted with, and the casual conversations and socializing on the job afforded me, and them, to get to know each other rather well before venturing out on a date. It worked out very nicely for me, and I had little trouble finding someone to go out with. And, knowing my predicament, there were a few occasions when my date offered to provide the transportation.

My weekend outing for August was a bus trip over to Toms River, New Jersey, for a visit with my step-sister Joan and her family. I had not seen them for awhile and I wanted to spend some time with them before the summer ended. I thoroughly enjoyed my time there, but I can remember thinking during the bus ride back that I would be glad when September arrived and the dances on Fridays resumed. I was now tiring of the jaunts from Wilmington over to the shore points on the Atlantic Ocean.

The dances that were so popular with us, and others, started up again in the middle of that month as anticipated.

Once again the four of us, Tom, Dave, Elmer and I would restart our regular attendance. I had no idea at the time that attending those dances would have long range consequences for me.

As fate would have it, or rather "someone's" sovereignty, the dance on Friday night, November 5th at the Lion's Club would change my life forever. But, it almost didn't happen, and yet it did happen; and I firmly believe that it was supposed to.

The fact is I didn't want to go to that dance. I had planned to hang-out at my apartment and just watch T.V. I had already bought my trusty six-pack of Schaefer's, and an assortment of "munchies." As I recall, I had just put in a difficult day on the job and didn't feel like getting dressed up and going out. However, my buddies had other plans for me. All three of them were relentless in trying to talk me in to going with them, almost to the point of badgering me. Finally, after being prodded for close to an hour, I relented and gave in to them. I was going after all. I asked them to give me a few minutes to shower, shave, and get dressed; which they readily agreed to do. With a grin, Dave said, "We'd be happy to wait for you, take your time." I don't know if there was an ulterior motive for that comment or not. I did notice, however, as we walked out the door, they had consumed my six-pack.

As was typical for most of the young men who attended these dances, the first destination when inside was directly to the bar. It must be what is commonly termed as a "guy thing", and every male seemed to always head in that direction, like a herd of cattle searching for the watering hole. We were no exception; it was the first stop the four of us made after entering the dance. Some guys called it "liquid refreshment", and some even referred to it as "liquid courage"; which I always thought was a sad comment to

181

be making. It denoted that particular young man had to have a few drinks before getting up the nerve to execute the simple task of asking a girl to dance. To be so devoid of any level of confidence seemed pitiful to me. For me, it wasn't a question of refreshment or encouragement, *I just liked to drink!*

There was nothing particularly unusual about the evening until the very end. It was the typical scanning over the girls, intermingled with the frequent trips to the bar.

I remember enjoying myself well enough, even though it took me awhile to snap out of my mood, and I was somewhat glad the guys had pestered me to join them for the night out. I finally admitted to myself that this was better than just hanging out, alone, in my apartment on a Friday night.

I danced enough, I drank enough, and I talked to enough young ladies during the course of the evening; enjoying myself doing so, but without any spark of interest in any of them.

It was about an hour before the dance was officially over that we all decided to call it a night. I can remember Tom asking me, "Gene! You ready to go?" "Yeah", I replied, "I guess I'm ready."

I wasn't.

I was making my way past the many tables, moving towards the exit, when for some *unexplainable reason* I felt an urge to look to my left. And there she was; this very attractive blond with long flowing hair.

I said, "Hey guys, hey guys, hang on a minute; I've got to check out this girl!" My buddies were very patient with me, the "minute" turned out to be over half an hour; but they didn't seem to mind, for they had simply meandered back to the bar.

I went over and asked the pretty blond for a dance and she accepted. We would dance a second time and then the remaining time left "on the half hour" was spent talking.

We learned that we had at least two things in common; the two of us regularly attended both of these popular dances, and we both worked for DuPont. And, somehow we got on the subject of Egyptology, which was probably more of an effort to keep the conversing going. Even so, I guess it was somewhat legitimate, for Carol and I still have an interest and fascination with ancient Egypt even to this day.

We also mentioned the upcoming dance, the "Bobalu", at the Fournier Hall, and asked each other if we planned to attend; our intention was we hoped to see each other again. There seemed to be a mutual desire in not allowing this initial interest in each other to just fade away.

I said goodnight and returned to collect my buddies at the bar, and we left for home.

On our way back to Wilmington, and the apartment, I tried to analyze and digest in my mind all that had just transpired. I was somewhat surprised at myself for venturing out of the protective shield I had placed around me so tightly; this was truly *a first* since my relationship with Margie had folded and was now history. There was something very different about this girl; there was an air about her, not arrogance, but a certain level of class in her demeanor. She could hold an intelligent conversation, was articulate in her speech, and just seemed to have a poise about her I had not seen in a girl for a long time. And of course, she was very, very attractive to me!

I was impressed!

I was interested!

I was glad I went to the dance!

And I am thoroughly convinced it was meant to be!

Also, I find it *extremely interesting* that I met both of the two most influential women in my life; one that I thought I was going to marry, and the one I did marry, at functions I *did not* want to attend!

It was almost as if I wasn't "calling the shots."

He who finds a wife finds what is good and receives favor from the Lord.

—Proverbs 18:22 (NIV)

I wouldn't say that I was preoccupied with my thoughts about this girl I had met at the dance throughout the whole following week, like some schoolboy infatuated with meeting his first girlfriend. However, I did find myself thinking about her off and on during that time, and the hope that I would see her again at the upcoming dance at Fournier Hall in Wilmington.

After Elmer and I arrived at the "Hall", and the dance that was "Bobalu" the following Friday night; I headed directly for "the watering hole", the bar, which of course was always my first "official" pit stop.

After acquiring my refreshment, I turned around to find an open table for me to sit, and immediately realized I couldn't move!

Unknown to me at the time, Carol had seen me come into the dance, and to make sure I knew that she was there, had moved over to the bar area and planted herself directly behind me. And there she was, she and her friend since grade school, Cathie Gracie, who were now essentially blocking my way. Carol didn't reveal to me until much later that this ploy was deliberate on her part, as she had an interest in seeing where this new development might lead. (What did I say before about women being devious?!)

We spent the better part of the evening together, mostly talking, and I imagine we were both exploring our own thoughts as to whether we "had something here"; or if it would turn out to be another one of those situations where, initially, things looked promising but for whatever reason the interest in the other party seemed to just fade away.

But it didn't fade away, for either of us.

Before the evening was over, I asked Carol if she would be interested in a date. She accepted, and our date the following weekend would commence a courtship which would culminate in our marriage on November 5th, 1966; exactly one year to the very day in which we had met. Next to my salvation she is the greatest thing that has ever happened to me, my "bright spot"—"the light of my life." We are presently in the 40th year of our marriage and I continually praise our Lord for bringing us together.

Following closely behind our relationship as a blessing is our three sons the Lord has given Carol and I; Michael, Gary, and Matt. They continue to be an incredible joy in our lives, and without question the Lord has honored us in our efforts to be good parents. All three of them are now in their 30's, well adjusted and industrious young men, gainfully employed and doing quite well for themselves.

How in the world did we do it!? How did we end up with such three fine young men; these three boys who never gave us any real trouble in raising them? Oh, there was the usual challenging of our authority from time to time; especially in those difficult years of adolescence, but what parent *hasn't* been through that? It's all but to be expected. Especially through that trying stage of being transformed from a child to a young adult; have we forgotten what that was like? And who in their right mind would want to go through *that* (adolescence) again!

But there have never been any problems with issues so many other parents have had to deal with; trouble with the law, trouble with drugs, and trouble *with girls*. Certainly the Lord has had His protective hand upon them, and they have, and continue, to honor us as their parents. Any success we may have had at parenting I simply but emphatically contribute to God's *grace*. Whenever we see other parents struggling with serious problems, such as already mentioned, Carol and I tend to take the old adage, "There but for the grace of God go I." Neither of us claim to have any unusual wisdom or design on parenting.

Still, there is one element that I do entertain that played somewhat of a factor; the differences in the experiences Carol and I had during our childhood. And we both learned from them. She knew what a real family was, and I knew what it *was not!*

She had a very positive family atmosphere, as opposed to the one I have already shared about concerning me.

Carol came from a very loving and accepting family. She claimed that although her father was strict, he was *always fair.* And mine, well, you already know about mine; but the fact remains that when our children were born I had no role model to follow, no point of reference. I never had a real father, and now I was one; *a fatherless father.* I essentially had to "wing it"; and any wisdom and insight, any expertise I might have had, I *MUST* contribute to the Lord's leading, for I know I didn't possess it on my own. I didn't know how to be the father I wanted to be, I just knew the father *I didn't want to be.* The Lord has honored and blest me in my efforts.

I am profoundly proud of our three sons; three good men, Michael, Gary and Matt; and they continue to honor me as their father.

<u>Matt</u> has told me and thanked me saying, "Thanks dad, for always being there for me."

<u>Gary</u> has said, "I don't know what I would do without you."

And <u>Mike,</u> the father of our grandson Josh, tells me, "Thanks for the role model you've been, I hope I am half the father to Josh that you've been to me."

Praise God! For, as a father, I must have done something right.

Sons are a heritage from the Lord, children a reward from him.

—Psalm 127:3 (NIV)

I Will Think Of You

For my wife, Carol.

Two hearts had been broken; one was yours,
the other one, mine.
Neither understanding why the love
we sought was so hard to find.
Perhaps we thought it was only a wishful dream;
a fairytale fantasy.
But the Lord had plans for us; and in time,
this we both would see.
For it has all been part of a design,
an exercise of His perfect sovereignty.
Your answered childhood prayer,
a "marriage made in heaven", and so it was meant to be;
that I found you, and you found me.
Ever so careful we were, right from the start.
Neither wanting to repeat the pain of a wounded heart.
But soon we would focus on each other,
and soon we would find; we two were falling in love,
leaving our pain and suspicions behind.
Many years have passed since our wedding day;
and I love and need you as much as ever,
more than anyone can say.
We've had that "marriage made in heaven",
had it right from the start.
Our love for each other grows stronger each passing year;
we're the keepers of each others heart.
And our love has produced three fine sons, whom
we dearly love; everyone can be sure of that.
Three good men, our three sons; Michael, Gary, and Matt.
And when both of us leave this fleeting life,
to be united with the Father and the Son.
We have nothing to fear, you and I; for death is but a brief
intermission, only an end to Part One.

And whoever might the Lord call first, we don't know; perhaps
me, or maybe you.
Either way, we will be reunited in the heavenly realms,
with the Lord our God, and our second life,
our eternal life—Part Two.
And, Ecclesiastes admonishes me to enjoy my life with my
wife, and this I surely do. For you are the light of my life, "my
bright spot", and I'm still in love with you.
So when my journey through this life is almost complete,
and my remaining thoughts are few.
I will think of the one who made my heart smile,
made my life worthwhile; and I will think of you.
Yes, Carol, my wife.
Carol, my life.
I will think of you.

CHAPTER TEN

SALVATION

FORGIVENESS

I fled Him, down the nights and down the days; I fled Him, down the arches of the years;

I fled Him, down the labyrinthine ways of my own mind; and in the midst of tears...."

So begins Francis Thompson's most famous poem "The Hound of Heaven", published in 1893 with a collection of his other works, simply titled "Poems."

It is written in the "old English" style, with words seldom, if ever, used in today's language and can be difficult to get through with any initial understanding. Even so, if one were to take the time to indulge in reading it, almost studying it, and pore over its meaning, it would soon become evident as to why it is considered a Christian classic.

Francis Thompson led a tragic life. He was born in 1859 to a respectable Catholic family, and at age eighteen would pursue becoming a priest, attending Ushaw College only to be dismissed by the headmaster; the only explanation being that "it is not the will of God that he should go on for the priesthood." He then spent the next six years studying to

191

become a doctor, only to fail the medical examinations three times. Some time during the interim he became addicted to opium. His family disowned him and he became destitute and homeless, living on the streets of London. It was there that he penned most of his works, including his 'classic.' His talent would go mostly unrecognized until after his death in 1907, at age 48, of tuberculosis and opium poisoning. In the three years after his death, his "The Hound of Heaven" alone would sell over 50,000 copies; and the publisher who owned the royalties would receive a small fortune. His funeral was attended by only a few mourners, none of which were family. And, curiously, by his own request, his epitaph reads; "Look for me in the nurseries of heaven."

His poem was very personal. He was penning his own salvation experience, that being of running from the Lord throughout the better part of his life, until he was finally "caught" by "The Hound of Heaven", namely, God.

I can identify with him, and his poem. Many people can.

For that is what we are, the natural man, we are runners! And if not runners, certainly ignorers. We have a natural inclination to go our own way, a propensity to pursue our own agenda in this life, ignoring the invitation of the Father to be restored into a relationship with Him through a personal faith in His son, Jesus Christ. To put it bluntly, we just don't have time for Him. I didn't! For so many years *I refused to listen* to the people He had brought into my life with the message of the Gospel, and restoration. I was, as we all are, rebellious in every sense of the word. I was the personification of what the scripture says about us, the natural man. The scriptures accurately describes my former state of ignorance and rebellion, and of all mankind; saying, "We all, like sheep, have gone astray, each of us has turned

192

to his own way; and the Lord has laid on him the iniquity of us all. Isaiah 53:6 (NIV). (ALL emphasis are mine.)

Another passage which correctly states the position of man from God's perspective is found in Psalm 53, where God says of us; "God looks down from heaven on the sons of men to see if there is any who understand, <u>any who seek God. Everyone</u> has turned away, they have together become corrupt; there is <u>no one</u> who does good, <u>not even one</u>." Psalm 53: 2, 3 (NIV) Take notice that it says "any who seek God."

It is not man who seeks a relationship with God, but rather God who seeks a relationship with us through restoration. To the unbeliever, all this 'religion stuff' is just so all unnecessary, almost fanatical. They conjure up in their own mind their own image of God, without investigating the scriptures to see what God has to say about Himself. They have their own personal perception, their own personal interpretation of who God is and what He is like. They are spiritually blind, and every bit the epitome of how the scriptures describe them when it says, "The man without the Spirit does not accept the things that come from the Spirit of God, for they are foolishness to him, and he cannot understand them, because they are spiritually discerned. 1Co 2:14(NIV). I know this to be true, for I used to be one of those people.

It is we who are lost, and it is God who seeks after us! It is proclaimed throughout all of scripture. It was God who sought out Adam and Eve after the fall, as they hid from Him in the garden. It is very the reason for the scriptures, the prophets, and the Messiah, Jesus Christ himself! The entire Bible speaks of restoration and is illustrated over and over in the scriptures.

For example, take a look at how many times the Jewish nation rebelled and turned away from God, only to be chastened, forgiven, and restored; but only after repenting.

And we are called to repentance today, through personal faith in Jesus Christ for the forgiveness of our sins. And, He, Christ, is the only way! The scriptures are very clear about this when it says of Him, "Salvation is found in no one else, for there is no other name under heaven given to men by which we must be saved." Acts 4:12 (NIV)

Jesus said of himself, "I am the way and the truth and the life. No one comes to the Father except through me." John 14:6 (NIV). And again in the book of Luke, Jesus says, "For the Son of Man came to seek and to save what was lost." Luke 19:10 (NIV) Notice whom it is that does the seeking; who does the saving, and the implication as to who is lost. We are!

And at this stage of my life I was still 'lost', but the Hound of Heaven of which Francis Thompson spoke of continued His relentless pursuit of me.

Carol and I were married in what I would now classify as a "secular Christian church." I use that phrase to describe a church that calls itself "Christian" and sounded like a church of the faith; but never presented the gospel message; personal faith in Jesus Christ alone as the only way of salvation. Sad, to be sure.

Even though we were not regular attendees, we had considered it to be our church, most likely because of our marriage there. Eventually our attendance would become even more sporadic, and in time would fade away all together. And, being somewhat judgmental, I consider these types of churches succinctly unfaithful, for they are unwittingly leading many astray, and giving a false sense of eternal security to those attending. Their standing is almost prophetic where the scriptures tell us; "There is a way that seems right to a man, but in the end it leads to death." Proverbs 14:12 (NIV).

Our decision to stop attending that particular church, however, was not based on any spiritual astuteness on our part, it was more of a result of a move. And, where we moved to, and where we still reside, was most definitely "a step directed by the Lord", as you will soon see.

We started looking for a home to purchase in the spring of 1968, although we had not originally intended to do so. Our plans were to save a considerable more amount of money to put as a down payment, and thus reduce our monthly mortgage payment as low as possible.. Unfortunately, the cost of new homes in the area were escalating faster than we could save, and we were saving an appreciable amount every month.

We had talked at great length during our engagement about our views on family life, and one of the major things we agreed on was, if at all possible, the mother should be in the home when the children arrived, to be there during the critical early formative years. Of course, in time our society and culture would change all this; not to mention what would become an economic necessity for two incomes to establish a home, but back during that time we still envisioned this attitude to be part of what was called "the traditional family practice."

With that in mind, we established right from the beginning of our marriage that we would live solely off my income and bank all of Carol's pay, saving it specifically for a down payment on our home. This would alleviate any great financial adjustment once we had our children, and it proved to be a wise decision on our part.

Carol would eventually have many different part-time jobs, contributing greatly to the family's budget, especially in regards to vacations; but she was traditionally home in the

195

mornings getting our three boys ready to go off to school, and then again when they got home in the afternoon. So as far as they were concerned mommy was "always" home.

We chose a home to our liking in a new development under construction known as Whitehall. As buyers, we had a choice between a typical three-bedroom split-level or a ranch model. Not particularly caring for the ranch, and perhaps the fact that "dad's" house was one, we opted for the split-level. Factored into that decision was my strong desire that our home include a garage, which the split-level offered and the rancher model did not. This was important to me so as to keep our car safe from vandalism. I had more than my fair share of those problems in the past; with hub caps stolen, a window shot out by a pellet gun, and a new convertible top sliced to pieces that was only two days old.

So, the split-level house we picked offered pretty much what we were looking for, both in design and affordability. Both Carol and I, individually, "always" liked this style of house, so it was easy for us come to an agreement to purchase what has now been our home for thirty-six years. Also, I firmly believe it is exactly where the Lord wanted us to be.

As most prospective homeowners do, we would take a ride to the site where our home was to be and check on its progress. Only two of the homes on our street were at the time completed and occupied, the rest of the twenty-or-so still in various stages of construction.

On one of our first visits to our lot we noticed another couple obviously checking on their property. The location of their house under construction made us realize we were to become neighbors, only four "doors" apart, and we walked down to introduce ourselves. Our neighbors- to- be were Walt and Flora Yarnall, originally from the Philly area. It would be the start of a friendship that lasts to this day, although great distance has separated us from interacting with each other as we had in the past. We have, however, been fortunate enough to visit them in the Phoenix area from time to time, and Flora and Carol regularly keep in touch via phone.

In time, after we had all finally moved into our homes, Walt and Flora would become involved in a local church known as Bethany Reformed Presbyterian Church, located only about seven blocks away. They attended church regularly; Carol and I did not. When we did go to church, which was very seldom, it was most likely the one I have already previously mentioned, the one we were married in.

All the new homeowners on the street who would become our neighbors seemed to move in approximately the same time, and just about every family on the street were young couples buying their first home. And like us, most of them had small additions to their families. Our addition was our firstborn son, Michael, approximately one-and-a-half years old.

We made settlement and moved in on March 1, 1969.

The landscaping which had been essentially completed by mid March needed much initial attention. This was particularly true in trying to coax the newly planted grass seed to properly germinate and take root. Watering the soon-to-be lawn, and the newly planted shrubs and trees was done almost daily. Many times this would cause the ground to settle, exposing a blanket of small stones that had found their way to the surface. This required an occasional careful light raking of the yard so as to leave only a smooth layer of topsoil.

One particular Saturday morning while performing this specific task, I noticed out of the corner of my eye someone approaching me from my right. I momentarily looked in that direction and immediately saw that this individual was carrying what looked to me like a Bible.

I did a double-take!

Not because I had noticed the Bible; but rather because *he* looked so familiar.

I can remember looking again in his direction, and thinking, "I know this guy; that's Leonard Edge!" We knew each other alright, and he instantly recognized me. With a smile and a warm welcome he shook my hand and said, "Hi, Gene; how are you?"

Leonard Edge was also from my home town of Prospect Park. He attended and graduated from what was then Prospect Park High School. But he had also graduated with my stepsister Joan. And unknown to me before that time, they had apparently dated for awhile during their school years.

He was also a member of "Bethany", the same church our friends down the street attended. He was touring the new neighborhood to invite people to the church, and if given the opportunity, take the time to witness to people who might be receptive to the gospel message and, of course, he had a "captive audience" in me.

He shared "the message" with me, and again, I just politely listened. I told him, 'I'll think on it." (I'm a hard sell!)

Our conversation over, he again shook my hand; and again invited me to church, and then went on his way. I stood there and just watched him walk down the street, somewhat dumbfounded that we would again meet up with each other; *especially* like this! I didn't quite know what to make of it. I remember pausing for a moment, thinking about the irony of it all, shook my head, and went back to work.

As our friendship with Walt and Flora became more solidified, they started to invite Carol and I to this local "Bethany Church" whenever they had some sort of social programs; Christmas and Valentines Day parties and other such gatherings. We enjoyed them so much, and the friendliness of the people, that we started attended the church services and became more involved with its people, establishing many friendships.

The church was pastured by the former Rev. Ray Wright, who also headed up a very committed visitation program. I am not sure how long Carol and I were involved with the church and it's people before "Pastor Wright" requested a visit to see us. I do know it took some scheduling and rescheduling until we could finally pull it off.

It was October 26th, 1972 when he, along with Elaine Ivory and Jim Powell, had their "visitation" with Carol and I at our home.

There was much good initial conversation; these people were very congenial and easy to like. They asked how we liked the church, the style of the Sunday service, and the people of the congregation. We also spent some time talking about the socials and the good times we had participating in them.

Then the obvious happened, the presentation of the gospel message; a *very thorough* explanation of God's plan of salvation for mankind; only possible by a personal faith in His Son, Jesus Christ.

Carol listened; I listened.

And now it was time for the invitation!

The pastor asked Carol if she was ready to ask Christ to be her Savior, to be forgiven of her sins; past, present and future, and to follow him as her Lord.

She responded with an enthusiastic, "Yes!" Then the pastor addressed me and asked, "What about you, Gene?"

I hesitated!

And hesitated!!

And hesitated!!!

Carol, somewhat frustrated and irritated with me, asked sharply, "Well, Don't you want to be saved?"

Instantly, I blurted out with a very profound and emphatic, "YES!"

I was *astonished, taken-back* by my unhesitant response. I was *genuinely surprised* at my own answer!

I can vividly remember asking myself, "Where did *that* come from; I said that?" It was if, and I believe to this day it to be so, the Holy Spirit had enough of my hedging; and that day, October 26th, 1972, at age 32, was going to be the day of my salvation. The scriptures says, indeed, Christ *himself* said; "All that the Father gives me __will__ *come to me, and whoever comes to me I will never drive away. John 6:37*(NIV).

It was the day of Carol's and my spiritual birth; because of the Grace of God the Holy Spirit, Christ's Spirit, resides in us and our salvation is secured. Praise God! That eventful day in October was the beginning of our second birth; the birth Christ spoke of in answer to Nicodemus's inquiries concerning the matter. Jesus speaks plainly and directly to the point in chapter three, verse three of John, where He says, "I tell you the truth, unless a man is born again, he cannot see the kingdom of God." Christ repeats the importance of the issue in verses six and seven; "Flesh gives birth to flesh, but the Spirit gives birth to spirit. You should not be surprised at my saying, "You *must* be born again." (Both verses from NIV).

And that simple but profound act of faith by Carol and I on that fateful day in October of 1972 would change our lives forever.

> For it is by grace you have been saved, through faith—and this not from yourselves, it is a gift of God—
> —Ephesians 2:8 (NIV)

I had a very difficult time in the early years as a new Christian. My initial joy and peace with this new found faith was quickly replaced with thoughts of doubt and suspicion. As many new Christians do, I found myself wrestling with the *assurance* of my salvation. I wanted to unquestionably believe what my standing in Christ was, but I could not. My quandary was of a different issue than the man mentioned in chapter nine of Mark where he says to Jesus, "I do believe; help me overcome my unbelief!" (NIV). He acknowledged the fact that he was struggling with the part of him that still had doubt; he didn't want to doubt, but he knew that it was there. That was my predicament for a long time, and I believe the deep seated cause for it was my poor father image.

The scriptures depict God as a caring, loving, and forgiving Father; something totally foreign to my thinking, nothing of which I had *ever* experienced with my earthly father, Bill Ling. The constant, unrelenting rejection and harsh treatment by him would not allow me to consider the possibility that God would accept me, certainly *not unconditionally!* I felt that I had to "walk the line", live an almost perfect life in order to "maintain" my relationship with Him. It was an erroneous picture of me holding onto Christ, and not the other way around.

It wasn't until I had studied the scriptures on the subject, and <u>believed</u> what God had to say about the matter that I finally found the peace I had been searching for; with Christ himself saying, "I give them eternal life, and they shall never perish; no one can snatch them out of my hand." John 10:28 (NIV) That, coupled with; "....nor anything else in all creation, will be able to separate us from the love of God that is in Christ Jesus our Lord." Romans 8:39 (NIV). Those two verses, *and my belief in them,* have forever resolved the issue.

Once a person becomes a Christian, and understands the magnitude of their forgiveness, they are then called upon to forgive others; something which can oftentimes be very difficult. For me, it was something I was readily willing to do; all for the exception of two people, Bill Ling and Irene B. Tunison. I just couldn't seem to let go of the memories of the years of rejection and abuse by my adopted father and grandmother. And, the truth is, I wasn't sure that I *wanted to.* Psychologically, there seems to be some sense of retaliation and satisfaction in continuing to cling to resentments; whether or not those feelings of retribution are real or only perceived. I just couldn't seem to take that difficult step of forgiveness towards these two people, it certainly wasn't something I was willing to initiate.

I didn't have to; God would set the course of events that would make it easier for me.

It was on a Sunday in June of 1976. Bill Ling called me to wish me "Happy Father's Day." I was taken back; but even more so by what followed. He went to great lengths to apologize to me, saying, "I'm sorry for not being the father I should have been." That is a direct quote, I have never forgotten it. It seemed that he was asking for my forgiveness.

I was so surprised I didn't know what to say. I recall just simply saying something like, "Well......., and then not really completing a sentence. I think at the moment I was questioning his sincerity; Bill Ling was not known for his truthfulness. Still, I knew there must have been some element of genuineness to it; for I know for a fact it was the *only* time I've known of him, or heard him, apologize to *anyone.* For him to admit a fault was totally out of character.

Without verbalizing it, I guess in my spirit I had forgiven him. We would embark on a new relationship, and even though it was much too late to develop a close one, it was definitely more than "civil"; one might describe it as somewhat of a congenial friendship.

I would eventually invite him and his new wife, Angie, down to our house for dinner; something I had previously vowed to myself that I would *never* do. He had thrown me out of his home, and I had been very adamant in my stand that he would never be welcome in mine. But something in me had changed, and I know who did the changing!

It would turn out not to be a one time event. He now was living with his new wife in Upper Darby, while renting his house on "Mad" Avenue, and invited me and my family up for dinner on many occasions. We started alternating these gatherings back and forth over the next few years of his life. I truly found myself enjoying them. Angie, of Italian heritage, always made us feel welcome and was a tremendous hostess. Also, for the very first time it seemed he was honestly interested in my opinions about various subjects and how things were going for me and my family. He may have been sincere, or not; perhaps "playing me", I had no way of really telling. I only know that I was cautiously willing to give him the benefit of the doubt. It was obvious to me as a believer this was the thing I was supposed to do. It didn't develop into a great relationship, but it was far better than it had ever been before. I really enjoyed the time we spent together; and although it would only last a couple of years, I was glad the differences between us had been resolved.

Bill Ling died of a massive heart attack at age 68 on Labor Day, the September of 1980. Ironically, his father Benjamin Ling had also passed away of a heart attack; on *Labor Day* in 1948! (Now, whenever Labor Day approaches I jokingly pretend to get a little nervous.)

At one point during his funeral, as Judy, Joan, and I were riding in the limousine, my twin sister and I found ourselves both weeping; neither one of us at first being able to understand why. He was never a real father to either of us; and Joan was there only as a matter of formality, there certainly was no "love lost" from her standpoint. I think she wanted to be there for Judy and me, nothing more.

It wasn't until later that Judy and I would discuss and explain our individual reasons why our response to "dad's" death turned out to be one of tears.

Judy shared with me that, for her, it was a sense of *relief,* not sorrow! As she put it, "I was finally rid of him." Her remarks may seem harsh to the reader, but *I know* they were justified.

My tears, however, were tears of profound sorrow; not from a sense of loss, but rather the realization that the only father I ever knew had absolutely no idea who I was, and it wasn't my fault. I was never allowed to show him, and he never took the time to find out.

I'm getting ahead of myself.

Before this all happened, there had been another event that had transpired.

As best that I can recall, my relationship with Mom-mom, such as it was, was re- established on her eightieth birthday, February 6, 1972. It would be another eight months before I became a Christian.

There was to be a huge celebration to acknowledge this milestone in her life, and of course, me and my family were invited. I wasn't sure I wanted to go, my memories of family gatherings were not pleasant ones. Even so, I knew that my name would be "mud" in the eyes of the other members of the family if I didn't show up. So, somewhat reluctantly, we attended the birthday party. It was a good decision.

All the family was there and it turned out to be a grand time, even for me.

It was the first real interaction I had with the family since the rift between me and my father got me thrown out of the house. The snide remarks I had been used to in my early years never materialized; I guess I had finally reached equal status with everyone else. The fact was that I had reached adulthood, and there was now the realization by certain others that any attack on my person would result in a immediate retaliatory response from me. I was now being treated with the common respect that had been denied me for so many years.

However, there was one incident during this celebration that I would savor for a long time to come.

Our firstborn, Michael, was now four years old; and this little guy was enjoying the party. He would gregariously make the rounds to all those attending, his friendly disposition delighting everyone. While seemingly having all the attention, someone remarked, "He's such a happy child." My immediate announcement was, "He should be, he comes from a happy home." It was a "dig", and I meant it to be. I was grinning, and aunt Bernice was smiling; she, if no one else, knew the intent of my remark.

There would be additional visits to my grandparents in the future; sometimes to specifically see them, other times just to stop by and say "hello" after visiting someone else.

On one such visit, awhile after Carol and I were Christians; my grandmother said to me as we were getting ready to leave, "I'd like to hear more about "your religion"; not now, but sometime in the future." Life is full of surprises, and that was one of them! She had obviously seen something different in us; certainly me, and she seemed curious as to how that came about. I saw it as an opportunity to witness to her, and I wasn't about to let it pass. "Sure", I said, "How about next week, next Saturday?" She agreed, and I had the whole week to pray and prepare for what it was I wanted to share with her.

I suppose the change the Lord has wrought in me has been plainly noticed by others; I can't see it, or at least not to a noticeable degree, but I guess it's there. As recently as eight months ago, while visiting my childhood friend Pat, to glean some information to be used in my book, he at one point asked me if I was as "still religious" as I used to be. I found the question to be almost comical, practically baffling, and I didn't know how to respond. Also, an elder and friend of mine from church, Don Jordan, and his wife Ruth, have both told me they have seen a great change the Lord has made in my demeanor; claiming that the once very evident angry disposition I once demonstrated is now gone. The scriptures say that I am "a new creature in Christ" and, apparently, I guess it shows.

I cannot understand why it seems the most difficult of all people to witness to are family, but it must be almost universally true, for I have heard it mentioned and discussed by many Christians before. Perhaps we are "too close", I don't know; haven't been able to figure it out. Strangely, though, I was hardly nervous at all when witnessing to this person who for so many years had been my nemesis. I guess my forgiveness to her was all but complete; if not, then why (I had asked myself) would I even be concerned about whether or not she was saved? Witnessing wasn't a matter of feeling obligated, although I was, (1 Peter 3:15) it was more of a sense of honor; to think the Lord would use the likes of me as an instrument to witness and perhaps bring someone to Christ. In my spirit I knew that not to move forward with this awesome opportunity would not only be an act of disobedience on my part, it would be an affront to the Lord; for the Christ who bled and died for me on the cross also bled and died for her. She needed to know this, and I needed to tell her.

On my drive back up to Pennsylvania the following Saturday I asked the Lord to give me not only the right words to say, but also a window of opportunity to say them. This alleviated any pressure on me to be preoccupied in trying to find the "right moment" in which to share my faith; I wanted the Lord to "orchestrate" this entire meeting. I can recall thinking, "This certainly has to be something He wants me to do, and if it is, He will give me the opportunity to do it.

He did.

Shortly after I arrived, Mom-mom offered me something to drink and I went to the refrigerator and claimed a can of soda. Returning to the living room, we started our conversation centered on the events of her birthday party, and how she now liked living on Prince Avenue, as they had sold their home on Summit Avenue and moved to the next borough, Norwood. We continued to chit-chat on various family related subjects and I made no attempt to steer the topic to that of religion. *She* opened the door to that subject by asking me, "Why is there all this sudden interest in religion." I don't know how she had determined there was, perhaps "dad" had mentioned something about it; or maybe it was the obvious new relationship between me and him that she had noticed. In any case, I distinctly remember thanking the Lord under my breath for opening that window of opportunity I had asked for.

I started out by telling her about my gnawing fear of death precipitated by Billy Fries's tragic accident. That, coupled with the annual paranoia that seemed to surface every summer due to the polio epidemics gave me little peace. I guess it could be seen as an unreasonable level of fear on my part, but it was real.

She claimed that she had never been afraid of dying, just viewed it as the natural order of things.

If I recall correctly, I then said something like, "Well, Mom-mom, what about after death, what then? Do you believe there is a heaven and a hell?"

She responded something like, "Well, I suppose there is, and, I know I haven't been perfect, but I know I'm not as bad as some people!" "That has to count for something!"

I explained (in a way that I have now forgotten) how God's criterion is not based on any kind of a merit system. His standard is *perfection; complete holiness,* something <u>totally unattainable</u> by mortal man. And yet we are <u>commanded</u> to be that way. I showed her what the scripture had to say about the matter and read to her 1 Peter 1:15 and Hebrews 12:14. There were of course many other related scriptures I could have used to impress the point, but I chose these two to refer to; stating clearly the issue at hand. I felt it somewhat prudent, knowing my grandmother, as not to seem too overbearing.

I then explained that God demanded a sacrifice for the forgiveness of sins (Heb 9:22) and the only sacrifice acceptable was found in the one He, God the Father, has provided for us in His Son, Jesus Christ; using the familiar verse from John 3:16. Faith in Him, Christ *alone,* as the way of our salvation; concluding my witnessing message with two verses, again from the book of Hebrews, Chapter 9, verses 27 & 28.

Mom-mom seemed to listen intently to everything I had to say and now it was time for the invitation. I simply asked her if she wanted to ask Christ to be her savior, to be forever free from the penalty of sin, and to trust Him alone for her salvation.

She kind of looked away from me for just a few seconds, apparently considering the offer just presented. She then turned back to me, looked me straight in the eye and said, "Yes, I do." I was elated, although not visibly showing it, and for a second I marveled at how our relationship had completely turned around.

I asked her to follow me in a simple "sinner's prayer" and heard with my own ears the one who had been my adversary for so long ask Christ to be her savior. I then turned to 1 John 5:13 and asked her to read it; she did so and just smiled.

Was her profession of faith sincere? I have no idea; the issue is ultimately between her and God. He is the only one who knew the condition of her heart, but my fervent hope is that it was.

I stayed for approximately another half hour, treating myself to another soda. My mouth seemed to be unusually dry, *Gee, I wonder why!*

After I had finished my refreshment, we said our good-bye's, I gave her a kiss, and headed for home.

I drove back down to Delaware with an incredible peace and joy in the knowledge of trying to serve my Lord.

> For my Father's will is that everyone who looks to the Son and believes in him shall have eternal life, and I will raise him up at the last day.
>
> —John 6:40 (NIV)

CHAPTER ELEVEN

FINDERS KEEPERS

In October of 2000, Carol and I joined Finders Keepers, one of the country's premier adoption search and support groups, located in Bear, Delaware. Its membership is typically described as a triad (although it is more than that) consisting primarily of adults who were adopted, birthparents who surrendered their children for adoption, and adoptive parents. Also involved in varying degrees are "significant others" (such as my wife), sibling searches, lost loves, grandparents, friends, classmates, etc. Unfortunately many people think it is an adoption *agency*, which it is not. The overall focus on the group remains to help the membership deal with the very personal issues and questions which arise from belonging to any one of those three main segments.

It was founded March 31st, 1988, by Ginger Farrow and Jean Manlove, both adoptive mothers. Ginger's initial reason for getting involved was to find medical information on her first husband who was himself an adoptee and had passed away; information critical to the medical history of her birth children. Indeed, that is a dilemma we adopted have faced our entire lives; not only do we not have a blood-line history, we have no medical history; something the medical profession has discovered in recent decades valuable to understanding their patient's health risks.

I have lost track of the countless number of times I have been asked to fill out a medical history background only to have nothing helpful to offer. Every doctor's office, hospital admissions cubical, employment application form; each requesting the same information, and me left without having *anything* meaningful to disclose.

"Is there a history of heart disease, hypertension, asthma, diabetes, (the list goes on!) in your family?" The answer is always the same, the simple and standard, "*I don't know!*"

We would have never known about "FK" if it had not been for Carol reading about it in a "general interest" article the Wilmington News Journal had printed. I had not read the coverage, but Carol suggested we inquire about the organization to see if we could possibly find any information about my background.

As usual, I was reluctant. I was now sixty years old and I figured too much time had passed to be able to dig up any meaningful information. Besides, I had tried that long ago to no avail. It was back in 1964, after I had first learned that Judy and I were adopted.

It didn't take me to be sixty years of age to figure out that I had approached it entirely the wrong way. Back then, in my naivety, and *anger,* I had presumptuously believed I could glean such information from the courts on my own. I figured I had *a right,* to know who my own natural parents were; after all, this is the USA, the land of the free, right?

I went to the courthouse in Media in my quest to find out who *I really was* and was totally unsuccessful. And it wasn't the fact that this then 24 year old had approached the issue in an entirely foolish way; rather it was the response from the courts representative that both hurt and infuriated me.

After explaining to a court clerk the reason for my visit and what it was I was trying to do, she responded by saying to me, *AND I QUOTE*, *"It's none of your business! As far as the court's concerned, the matter is closed. You have not right to any information!* My incredulous response was, *"What! This is crazy!"* Her answer was simply, "I'm sorry, we can't do anything for you. I left frustrated and angry; and that experience was my reasoning for not pursuing the matter any further.

But as usual, I have a propensity to find out the many things I don't want to do are precisely the things I should do. A party and a dance had already proven that point.

As circumstances would play out, it was the finding of a letter from "dad's" papers after his death that would prompt our involvement with Finders Keepers.

Carol had been in the process of straightening up our basement when she came across a box containing papers that had been in our possession since his death in 1980; I had just never deemed it important to go through them. I figured that I would eventually do so but I didn't see a need for any great hurry. Bill Ling was a very secretive, private individual, and I didn't really believe there would be anything of real interest in the box.

Then I found it!

The only really worthwhile information was a letter in response to one our grandmother (Mom-mom) had written to Crozer hospital concerning our birth. She needed to write a letter to the Pennsylvania Department of Vital Statistics to obtain an updated birth certificate for my sister and I; required to be able to enroll us in school.

The letter says, "Eugene Carroll Hall, Jr. and Judith Lee Hall were born in J. Lewis Crozer Hospital Chester, Pa. on Jan. 16,1940. The father's name was Eugene Carroll Hall and the mother Theodora Estelle Killem (Maiden name). The "Killem" was a "typo" and should have read Kille<u>n</u>.

We now had a name to work with, a starting place, that would eventually lead us to the information that would clear up the questions we had been desperately trying to find answers to for so many years. And it was Finders Keepers and Ginger Farrow who would show us and guide us on how to do this. Ginger seems to thrive on this sort of thing, and it was her industriousness and dedication that finally resulted in so much information for Judy and I. And I also believe that us finding out about this group, and our involve- ment in it, was by no accident.

Ginger's expertise acquired from over seventeen years experience gave me a wealth of ideas and direction in how to approach my search. Guided by her, I now solicited the courts in Pennsylvania in the proper manner. Step by step, in a very precise sequence, she taught me what documents to petition for and how to do it. Also, she guided me to The Delaware County Historical Society in Broomall (PA.) which held a wealth of useable data in which to use, opening methods of searching I had no idea existed.

Later on, I would learn enough to enable me to conduct some searching on my own; eventually impressing her to the point where she teasingly remarked that she ought to hire me!

Apparently the high point of the membership at one time was sixty-three, with thirty or so attending the meetings on a fairly regular basis. The current membership is now considerably less, evident of the continual flux of the number of participants. For whatever reason, after many of those involved find the info they had been looking for, they tend to drop out. I guess our group had served their purpose and now was no longer needed. For the rest of us there is an obvious well-establish friendship, and even though there are times when we don't meet as often as in the past, we all seem to come together on somewhat of a regular basis.

Ginger tells me she is searching all the time, it never ends. After asking her how many searches she has done over all those years, she told me that she didn't have an actual count, but *she does* have <u>nine cabinets</u> filled with files!

> In his heart a man plans his course, but the Lord determines his steps.
>
> —Proverbs 16:9 (NIV)

REUNIONS:
ADOPTIVE FAMILY

BIRTH FAMILY

Once we knew the truth about our adoption, a truth divulged by our Aunt Anna, Judy felt for her own peace of mind the necessity to find the answers to two gnawing questions that continually troubled her.

With our history of being constantly fed a steady diet of "deceit and lies" it was extremely important for her to try and extract those answers from Mom-mom; knowing that it would be hopeless trying to confront dad.

Both she and Joan have often remarked, "You can never tell if he's lying or telling the truth.", so Mom-mom was her best bet in an effort to get those questions resolved.

Indeed, the one time I was able to confront Bill Ling about our adoption, and our biological parents, his explanation to what had happened to them was, "they were both killed in an automobile accident", which turned out to be a flagrant lie.

Our grandparents move from Prospect Park to Norwood and the proximity to where Judy and her family lived gave Judy the opportunity to visit them often.

217

On one such visit, and knowing she shouldn't press Mom-mom too hard, she said to her, "I need to know the answer to two questions, _just two;_ but I need to know the _truth!_"

"Is it really true that Gene and I were adopted, and is Gene _really my brother?_"

Mom-mom's answers were in the affirmative for both of those issues Judy was struggling with, and about the only other information our grandmother offered freely about our mom was in reference to my relationship with her. She said, "Gene and Betty really bonded together, they were very close." That revelation to me may be why I seemed to miss her so much, and may very well be the reason for some of the abuse. "Dad" had been hurting over the breakup of his marriage to Betty, and when Mom-mom looked at me, she saw the hurt she had caused her dear son, and resented it.

There must have been something to her statement in reference to the "bonding", for I have often thought about our mom, and whatever happened to her, on and off through- out my entire life.

We knew her maiden name was Taylor, but we didn't know if she had reclaimed that name after divorcing Bill or if she kept the name Ling. Also, she was still a young woman at the time of their divorce and it was certainly reasonable to assume she had remarried. We had no name or location, basic information in which to start a search, and finding her was all but impossible.

By the way, Judy has had a lot of fun "bragging" to her friends and co-workers that our mom was Elizabeth Taylor; causing much laughter in response.

My wife Carol is now in her twentieth year as the office manager for Harris Jewelers in Bear, Delaware.

In February of 2001 a customer in the store mistakenly thought she had known my wife from someplace before. The customer looked at Carol and said, "You look so familiar, do you know me?" Carol responded that she was certain that she did not. Undaunted, this lady then asked, "What's your name?" (Later this person would say she *never* asks questions like that, and really doesn't know why she had this time) Carol's reply was, "Well, my married name is Ling, Carol Ling."

The customer just looked at her, and after a short pause said, "I know the name "Ling", but the only Ling I knew was a Bill Ling who was married to my aunt Betty, and they adopted two children, Judy and Gene." Carol's response was, "Well, Gene is my husband!"

This lady's name was Bobbi Koukoulis, our adoptive cousin, who used to frequently baby-sit Judy and I when we were infants; and our 56 year separation from our mom was about to end.

Carol's co-workers knew of my background through various conversations over the years and they seemed to be fine-tuned to the verbal exchange Bobbi and Carol just had; and probably were as dumbfounded by the turn of events as much as Carol was. Even to the point where the store manager, Ken Scott, said something to the effect of, "This is crazy, this isn't supposed to happen!"

Carol and Bobbi retired to the back of the store where they cried and talked. They "compared notes" as to where they had both worked over the years, social events, other people they knew, and the possibility they may have met each other through them. Nothing! "We realized we really didn't know each other", Carol said. She continued, "This has got to be God; there is no other way to explain it."

After talking with each other for just a few minutes, Carol called me at home.

When I answered the phone she was crying and right away she said to me, "Sit down, I have something to tell you!" Naturally, I was alarmed, her state of mind signaled to me that something was very wrong. I was immediately concerned it might be about one of our three sons. I anxiously asked, "Is it one of the boys, are they okay?!"

She assured me right away that they were fine; then continued to explain what had just transpired. After realizing what I had just been told, I asked, "Can she stay there?" "I want to come down to see her." She agreed to wait for me and I rushed upstairs to recover the only photo I had of our mom, then left quickly for the store.

When I arrived, and with tears in her eyes, Bobbi gave me a big hug and asked, "Do you remember me?" Of course, I didn't; I was much too young to be able to recall any memories of those very early years. I showed her the picture I had brought with me, and she spontaneously said, "Yep, that's my aunt Betty!"

The three of us sat in the office area in the back of the store and talked. Bobbi said how she used to take the bus down from Philadelphia, walk the three blocks to our house to baby-sit us; the three of us often playing in the backyard. She also said I had something of an appetite for worms; I would dig them up and eat them, and probably explains a few things about myself as far as some idiosyncrasies that are exclusively mine.

Then at some point in our conversation I had to ask the obvious question, "Is our mom still alive?" Bobbi responded, "Yes, she lives in Florida, outside Tampa in an area called Largo." As it would turn out our son Gary lived only about thirty miles away from her, and he would be the first to be reunited with our mom, and his grandmother.

Bobbi asked me if I wanted to contact her. My automatic reply was yes; with the understanding that if our mom didn't want to be reconnected it was alright. I acknowledged the fact that so much time had passed and at her age perhaps she wouldn't want to. I understood that; and made sure Bobbi realize I wouldn't push the issue.

She said she would call that evening, a Tuesday, to inform our mom of the events of that afternoon. That night Carol and I waited at home in anticipation of a phone call.

The evening came and went without the phone ringing. I wasn't concerned about it though, reasoning the news for mom had to be somewhat of a shock and surprise, and she was now trying to mentally process this new development in her life and decide what to do with it.

I stayed home all day Wednesday to make sure I wouldn't miss a phone call if there was to be one. Still, there was no call.

Wednesday evening; again, nothing!

Thursday I stayed around the house all morning, waiting; then decided Judy should know what was going on. I wanted to tell her in person, so I drove up to Norwood.

We sat at her dining room table and she was wide-eyed as I told her the news. Her mouth was gaping open and finally shook her head and said something like, "I don't believe this, this is incredible!" We both shared our fascination about this turn of events after so many years had passed without being able to find out *anything* about our mom.

I had stayed at Judy's much longer than I had intended, so I thought it prudent to call Carol back in Delaware, to make sure she knew I was okay and I wouldn't be staying much longer before traveling back home.

Carol had just returned home from work when I called and she said to me, "Come home now; there's a message for you on the answering machine!" When I told Judy this, she said something to the effect, "Go, Go!" "Be careful going back, and *call me* as soon as you can!" I hastily made my way back to Delaware, and home.

Carol was as excited as I was; although I was somewhat apprehensive as to what the message was, for I wasn't quite sure what to expect.

Carol met me at the curb when I pulled up in front of the house. When I got out of the car I said to her, "You know, I don't know what to call her; in my heart I want to call her *mom,* but I don't know how she will respond to that after all these years." Exasperated, Carol again repeated, *"Go listen to the answering machine!"*

Carol followed me upstairs to our bedroom and sat beside me as I took a deep breath and pressed the button on the answering machine. I then heard a voice that I had not heard for fifty-six years say to me, "Hello, this is your momma calling from Florida."

Carol and I just sat there, both weeping, and not saying a word. It wasn't until then I realized the profound impact she must have made on me. Psychologically, I must have had a great need for that relationship between mother and child in those all important early years. I needed a mother in my young life, and I never had one.

After we composed ourselves I got on the phone and called Florida. My initial conversation with mom was a delightful one, and to this day I believe her voice sounded vaguely familiar to me; even after all those years. By the way, I still have the recording tape from the answering machine when our mom first called. *No way* is that message going to be erased!

In the course of our conversation I informed mom that she had one of her grandsons living not far from her. I told her his name was Gary, our second born, and lived only about forty minutes away from Largo. I asked her, "If he was up to it, would you like to hear from him?"; but also stipulating that he might feel a little uncomfortable and not really want to. (Gary, at this time, had no idea as to what had transpired).

Mom was delighted at the idea!

I called Gary almost immediately after my conversation with my mom and filled him in on all the details. Naturally, he was surprised. Then he surprised me! I wasn't really sure if I should suggest to him to call her, knowing it could seem to be very awkward for him, but he readily agreed.

Another forty-five minutes passed when Gary then returned a call to us. He said to me, "Dad, she's so friendly; it's like I've known her all my life."

I was ecstatic!

Then he said, "She's already invited me to dinner, but I don't know what to do." "What do you mean?" I responded. He replied, "Well I don't know if I should really see her *before you do!*" I knew that he was trying to be considerate and I appreciated it, even so, I said, "*GARY! Go see your grandmother!*

He did.

Now it was time to call Judy. She was thrilled at all that had transpired and almost immediately we entertained the idea of a trip to complete our reunion. And this we did; the three of us, Judy, Carol, and I started planning a trip to Florida. We didn't want to "drag our feet" on this one; mom was now in her eighties, and it would be prudent for us to try and see her as soon as we could, acknowledging that none of us knew what the future holds. After all this time, it would be terrible not to be able to visit and talk with her should "something happen."

After conferring with our mom, we settled on a date of March first for a reunion visit. Gary had now visited with his grandmother and said he thoroughly enjoyed himself. He also said mom had packed "a bunch of goodies" for him to take back home.

I should interject here at this point the reason why several days had passed before our mom had made contact with us.

She had never told her husband, Paul Jump, or our brother Gregg about Judy and me. Gregg was also her adopted son, mom never having natural children of her own. She needed time for Gregg and his wife Patty to make the three hour trip up from their home in the Lake Okeechobee area before she revealed this part of her past to the three of them, and she wanted to do this in person and not by phone. Understandably, they were surprised, Gregg making the comment, "Momma, you really know how to keep a secret!" I surmise the reason she had never said anything was because it was so far in her past and it was really not necessary to bring it up. Our relationship was all but "history" and, like us, she never really expected to ever see us again.

Carol was working the day I went to see our travel agent at the AAA office in Newark to make arrangements for the three of us to fly to Tampa on March 1st.

I specifically requested to see Colleen McKeown, an employee who had made many travel arrangements for Carol and I in the past; a very knowledgeable and capable agent, so much so that Carol and I had dubbed her "our agent", laying somewhat of a personal claim to her.

As I was explaining the urgency of our trip on such a short notice, and sharing my story with her, her eyes were glassy as she typed away on the computer searching for air travel for the three of us. Then she shook her head and said, "I don't believe what I'm seeing here."

"What? What's the matter?" I inquired. "Well", she said. "There's just two flights leaving from Philadelphia to Tampa on the day and time you want to go." The first flight is completely booked; and the second flight has only *three* seats left! You won't be together, but you'll all be on the same plane!"

I said, "We'll take them!"

I believe, in the sovereignty of God. *I believe,* that He is in control; and nothing touches me without first passing through His hands. *I believe,* He knows what we have need of before we ask. (Matt. 6:8). And regardless of what anyone else may think, *I also believe,* those three seats were set aside for us back in 1945!

Is that a foolish statement to make?

Is it?

Does God *really* know the end from the beginning; or to pose the question in another way, is there *anything* that can take God by *surprise?* Does He *really* know what is going to happen before it does? Did not Jesus tell Peter he would deny Him three times <u>before</u> the rooster crowed?

I rest my case.

Judy and I scrambled to contribute photos we individually owned and hurriedly put together a scrap book of our years growing up together, to present to our Mom during our first visit. We wanted to try to give her some indication of our development during all those years she was denied a relationship with us.

Carol would turn out to be our "official reporter", documenting the events of our reunion on a video recorder we had borrowed from our niece, Dawn Williams. That, along with the prolific clicking of my Nikon, would ensure a wealth of visual memory makers.

We rented a car at the Tampa airport and stopped along the way to purchase some flowers before continuing on to Largo. Gary was at work on this particular Thursday and would join us that evening for dinner. Gregg and Patty would make the drive up from Lake Okeechobee on Sunday, and Judy and I would finally meet our brother.

We had no sooner pulled up to the curb at their home in the trailer park when we saw an elderly woman, obviously our Mom, walking down the driveway to meet us. Judy was first to greet her, and mom immediately held Judy's face in both hands, and with tears in her eyes said, "There's my daughter." Carol was busy with the video camera, recording this most important occasion, and I was grinning from "ear to ear". All of us were teary-eyed.

My first words to her were, "Hi, Mom, How are you?" followed by a warm hug and a kiss. I then introduced our Mom to Carol and they also greeted each other in the same manner. We then went inside to meet her husband Paul.

Paul Jump was a very gentle man; very friendly and easily likeable. Unfortunately, he was also in very poor health, being afflicted with both Parkinson's disease and Multiple Sclerosis. Right away, he asked if it would be okay for us to call him "Pop"; the indication being clear that we were both welcome and accepted. I think my response was something like, "Sure, Pop; that would be great." It was the beginning of a terrific weekend.

Mom had apparently shared this new development in her life with her many friends and there were visits on and off throughout the day to meet "the twins." We talked and talked, there was much catching up to do. We conveyed the fact that we could never find out anything about her. She shared that she had often called the house to talk to us but there was always some excuse; we weren't home or "in for a nap", constantly being refused any contact with us. She also revealed she had sent cards and gifts on our birthdays and at Christmas, none of which we ever received.

Judy disclosed the incident when she first suspected we might have been adopted; I shared the interview I had with the officer in the Air Force and the first time I heard the word "adoption." Carol related the story about her and

Bobbi in the store and how that started the events we were now sharing. Judy and I went through the photo album with Mom and explained the many photos which was essentially our entire childhood and teenage years; and through it all Carol kept the camera rolling. And of course, without Mom going into any great detail, she touched on some of the abuse she had suffered and the need to end her marriage to Bill Ling. Both Judy and I could relate to her story and we understood.

Sunday arrived and so did our brother Gregg and his wife Patty. I have to admit that I was a little apprehensive about this meeting. I wasn't sure how this person had taken the news about our existence, and the idea he was now going to have to share some of the attention from Mom that had been exclusively his for so many years.

My fears were totally unfounded. All five of us; Carol, Judy, Gregg, Patty and I, "hit it off" very well; and in the few years that have transpired we have *truly* bonded together. The three of us have made several visits back to Florida since our initial reunion, with Gary oftentimes joining us after work; visits totally enjoyed by all.

The "girls"; Mom, Judy, Carol, and Patty; have enjoyed doing the "flea market thing", while Gregg would take me out on the lake on his air boat; just a few examples of our time together.

Gregg, like me, is now retired. His profession was one of being a fishing guide for sportsmen desiring to fish Lake Okeechobee. He was so proficient at what he did that he earned the reputation for being the best guide on the lake, being in great demand.

His clientele have included celebrities such as Paul Newman and Anthony Hopkins.

Mom has also visited here in the area to spend some time with her brother who resides in Aston, Pennsylvania.

And that particular visit was an opportune time for her to meet her other two grandsons, our sons, Matt and Mike. She also got a chance to meet her great-grandson Josh.

The experience of that reunion in March of 2001 has been very therapeutic for me; answering some very difficult questions that had plagued me for so many years. It has also revealed and disclosed to me some issues I had with the whole scenario pertaining to our adoptive parents divorce. Questions in my thinking as to why things had played out the way they had; and an understanding of the reason for them. Questions and answers I have shared with Carol and my sister alone; not to be discussed with anyone else.

Our initial visit was capped-off by an article written by Berlinda Bruce, a reporter for the "Delaware People" section of The Wilmington News Journal, Delaware's statewide newspaper. Appropriately enough, it was published in The Sunday News Journal on Mother's Day, May, 2001.

It was a tremendous reunion, a fantastic development in the lives of my sister and me. But it wasn't the only reunion that would take place in 2001; there was to be another.

That one would be in June, and would require a trip to North Carolina.

> Give thanks to the Lord, for he is good; his love endures forever.
>
> —Psalm 118:1

Ginger has all but perfected the method in which to conduct an adoption related search. Through many years of experience she has formulated a step-by-step process that has, for the most part, proven to be extremely successful; not fool-proof, but her success rate certainly gives evidence that it works.

There are many people within our organization that are forever indebted to her for her assistance in finding biological family, two of which are my sister and I. Her tutoring has been extremely helpful to me in learning not only what questions to have answered *first,* but also how to *ask those questions* to authorities in a very *particular* way.

I have learned much from her, and what I have learned has been instrumental in "picking up the ball"; to be able to search entirely on my own, and eventually *find our father,* Eugene Carroll Hall! Ah! But once again, I get ahead of myself!

Through Ginger's guidance, and very active participation, I have been able to acquire copies of our adoption papers, our mother's death certificate and obituary, and information from the funeral home that handled her funeral.

It should also be said that she has certain "tricks of the trade" that she will not divulge to the rest of us; "trade secrets", if you will. She obviously has some connections that have all but sworn her to secrecy; and it would be prudent for her continued success as a searcher to honor those promises.

I don't recall *exactly* when Ginger contacted me for an all important phone call, but I put it sometime before early May because I know it was before the "Mother's Day" article in The News Journal.

When I answered the phone on that particular day she said, "Gene, hold on; I have somebody on the line and we're going to have a conference call." A few seconds went by and I heard her say, "Ok, go ahead." A third voice said to me, "Hi, this is Lana, your cousin." This was the start of being reunited with *birth family!*

Ginger had used her refined techniques and found our biological cousin, Lana Gentile, and her mother, our Aunt Esther, in Old Fort, North Carolina. Our Aunt Esther was sister to our <u>mother</u>, Dora Killen Brinton Hall! My brain was totally scrambled at this extraordinary development, so much so that I do not clearly recall much of the original conversation; my mind being in sensory overload! However, one of the things I DO remember, and probably because it meant so much to me, was that Judy and I obviously had not been forgotten by the family. Lana said her mother would often talk about "the twins", and the fact that she had shown an interest in adopting her sister's children herself. The problem was they couldn't find us, even after hiring a detective to try and do so. Apparently, as mentioned before, our actual adoption had been "signed, sealed, and delivered" <u>so quickly</u> that Judy and I had just "vanished into thin air."

Naturally for me there was now an urgency to be physically reconnected with our blood relatives, and immediately we started formulating plans for another reunion visit. This one was to take place in early June; and Carol, our son Mike, and I headed for Old Fort, just outside of Asheville, North Carolina. Judy would not make this trip with us, having other definite plans she was already committed to. It would be the following year that she and Lana would finally meet.

We stayed in a motel Lana had suggested, relatively close to her and her husband's home up in the mountains.

This was probably a good thing since we soon realized we would have never found it on our own, having followed them there after our dinner.

Lana specifically picked this motel for us as it was located next to a nice restaurant where we would have the dinner just mentioned.

After calling and informing them we had arrived in the area, they left their home in the mountains and arrived at the motel approximately twenty minutes later. We were waiting for them outside the door of our motel room when they drove up. The first words I heard from Lana were not directed towards me but instead to her husband Ken. All three of us heard her distinctly say to him, while looking at me, "He's a Killen!" Sweet words to me for sure.

Waiting inside their vehicle was the sixth member of our party, the sole living person that was closest to my mother, my Aunt Esther. And even though she was afflicted with that dreaded disease we know as Alzheimer's, a disease that robs the elderly of the memories that is their life, it was an incredible blessing to meet her, something that I will always cherish.

Lana would tell us it was a shame we hadn't been able to connect with each other about ten years before we did, her mother had at that time a very sharp mind and would have been able to share much information about the many stages of our mother's life.

But, it just wasn't meant to be. I was okay with that; I was thankful for what I had, and it was so much more than I ever had before.

This reunion was very beneficial to Lana also, as she was very much into genealogy and this situation was going to add a whole new chapter to her findings. Also, she has been obviously very appreciative of finding blood relatives; Judy and I are now the last remaining two that she has. Our Aunt Ester, and Lana's mother, passed away on April 4, 2004.

Ken and Lana did everything to convey they were as happy about this reunion as we were. Again, as with the other occasion, there was a lot of picture taking, sharing of personal histories and backgrounds, and this first night was celebrated with the presentation of a bottle of champagne and a cake. I smiled as I read the message on the cake which said, "Welcome back to the family." Needless to say we consumed both.

Sometime during the next day the question of photographs of our parents came up, a definite interest for Judy and I in obtaining some of them if there were any available. Ken had already done a thorough search of family memorabilia stashed in many boxes stored in their garage attic; but to no avail. There was none to be found of our parents, Eugene and Theodora Hall. Still, Lana was convinced her mother must have had some stored around *somewhere*, and finally remembered her mother had a few photo albums in a bottom drawer of one of her dressers. There were five of them, and Carol, Mike and Lana started looking through them. I was out on the porch taking photos *of photos* that were part of the family's history, but unrelated to the purpose of our visit.

It wasn't until they were going through the last and final album that Mike came out onto the porch and exclaimed, "Dad, you've got to come in here, quick!"

I went to the table, and with Carol intently watching my reaction, saw a photograph of a man with the name "Gene Hall" written above it! A few moments later, and another picture appeared; and that one had a woman standing next to him. Above the picture were the names, "Gene" and "Dora." I finally knew what my birth parents looked like; I was sixty-one years old.

Ken promised he would get copies made for me, duplicates, a complete set for both Judy and I. This he did, and we received them by mail shortly after we had arrived back home in Delaware.

In a very short period of time, I met up with Judy to give her the copies that were to be added to her collection of all the documents I had found.

Judy has always claimed that she may very well forget someone's name, but she _never, ever_ forgets a face! She paused just for a second after looking at our father's picture, and then with her mouth half opened exclaimed, "That's Ray!"

She is very adamant in her belief the man that we used to tidy ourselves up for, the one we would run up to the apartment to see, dad's "friend", was indeed "Eugene Carroll Hall", _our father!_ To this day she believes it to be so. I, on the other hand, remember the visits, but I simply do not remember the face.

All the information we have attained has answered a host of questions for us about our birth family and adoption. There are still many questions that remain, but we are sensible enough to recognize that in all likelihood they will go unanswered. For the most part, Judy and I are pretty much satisfied with what we have. At the time, though, there were only two more critical questions we needed to have answered. Where was our mother's final resting place, where was she buried; and what had happened to our father?

The first questioned would be answered on May 21, 2001, just a few weeks before our trip to North Carolina. The second one would take much more time.

Judy, Carol, and I spent a lot of time roaming the graveyards of Delaware County, Pennsylvania, looking for headstones with the name HALL engraved on them. We searched cemeteries in Boothwyn, Concord, Linwood, Chichester,

Aston, and others I can no longer recall. In almost every case we found a very large number of "Halls", but no Dora or Eugene. We did not know during this long, arduous, time consuming searching that we were looking in both the wrong places and for the *wrong name.*

Then on May 21st, for whatever reason, a reason I have only explained to others as "a gut feeling", I decided to look for our mother at the same cemetery Agnes Ling was buried in, Lawncroft Cemetery, in Linwood, PA. Judy would say at a later time, "That would have been the last place I would have looked." Her reason being that most of the family was from the Rockdale area of Aston Township, with a long history of residency there; and most were buried in the surrounding graveyards, several miles from the Lawncroft site.

It is amazing how a little piece of information can beget more pertinent information, and *that* information can lead to still more; the data then seemingly to "snowball." This is the very real reason POW's are instructed to give only their name, rank, and serial number to their interrogators; anything more might lead to divulging sensitive material useful to the enemy.

Our mother's death certificate provided me with the information I needed to do a concentrated, well focused search. Nominal information, it would seem, data initially overlooked, but once found would allow me to focus on a well defined time frame.

Not only did her death certificate have our mother's birth and death dates, it also included her actual *burial* date and the name of the funeral home involved. I could now canvas whatever cemeteries I chose, armed with a specific burial date. I reasoned their records would easily tell me if there was a funeral at their cemetery on that particular date, and whose funeral it was. I was looking for a funeral on February 7th, 1942— Dora Hall's. With the advantage of this information, my first stop after arriving at Lawncroft would be the office building. There I spoke with an elderly clerk who was both helpful and person- able.

I told her who I was looking for; a Theodora or "Dora" Hall, buried on the 7th of Feb. I also stated that she was my birth mother, and other tidbits of my story, and that I wasn't even sure she was buried there. The sharing of some of my story was an effort to tweak her interest. I was successful; I got her attention. It seemed to me that, for her, this was one of the more interesting assignments she had come across for awhile, and she was now very methodically searching the records.

I noticed her head moving back and forth from side to side, intently examining a large index card. She then said, "No, there were no Halls buried at this location on that day. As a matter of fact our records indicate there is no Hall family plot at this location at all." There was a brief pause then she said to me, "Does the name *Killen* mean anything to you? There was a Dora Killen buried here on that date." Now she had <u>my</u> attention; I had found our mother! "Yes", I said excitedly; "That was my mother's maiden name!"

"Well", she responded, "There is a Killen family plot here; let me go in the back for a minute and then I can find the exact location for you." As she left for the backroom I was finding it difficult to contain myself, I felt like shouting! I can specifically remember thanking the Lord under my breath; for it was obvious to me He was continuing to open doors of information for us.

She returned with a complete map of the cemetery rolled up like a scroll. After comparing the notes on the index card with the map, she was able to pinpoint the section and location of the Killen family plot. I thanked this kind lady for her most appreciated help, said goodbye, and left the office for the burial site.

As it would turn out, our mother shares a grave with an infant Killen, Elizabeth Killen, our Uncle James' daughter, who passed away at age four. There is a full-size casket underneath this child that holds the remains of our mother.

The grave marker noted the burial site of this little child, but there was nothing to indicate the presence of another; our mother had rested in an unmarked grave for almost sixty years. This was totally unacceptable to Judy and I. We have since placed a bronze marker on her grave. It reads, "Mother", Dora Killen Brinton Hall, Feb.5, 1911-Feb.3, 1942; "We Shall Meet Again."

When I visited my mother's grave for that very first time on that special day, May 21st, 2001, I found that I could not cry, and I didn't want to. I was so glad we had finally found our Mother; I was happy. I simply said "Hello Mother, this is your son Gene Hall; how I would loved to have known you." I was smiling.

I then glanced across the cemetery grounds to the final resting place of Agnes Ling, just a little over one-hundred feet away. How could I have ever known that I was ever so close to our mother, just thirty-eight years before; standing there at Agnes's gravesite as a pallbearer.

I marveled, and wondered, at the twists and turns my life has taken.

Praise be to the Lord God, the God of Israel, who alone does marvelous deeds.
—Psalm 72:18

CHAPTER THIRTEEN

EUGENE CARROLL HALL OUR BIOLOGICAL FATHER AND HOW I FOUND HIM

A ream of copy paper is usually a 500 sheet count. It took me in excess of 654 sheets to find our biological father, Eugene Carroll Hall. I know it was at least that number because I counted them; and a very conservative estimate of those sheets discarded which yielded no pertinent information could easily bring the count to well in excess of 750.

The amount of time spent in this monumental task I put at a minimum of 80 hours, and that was *just to find him;* and to acquire the additional information that I would find entailed continuing my search for months; those total hours being much too difficult to estimate.

I will now go through the process which I used to get that information, the reason being twofold.

First, it will demonstrate how I did it, and illustrate what I have already alluded to in the previous chapter; how seemingly sparse information is often times enough to acquire the tools to expand on that information, the "snowballing" effect, if you will. Secondly, it may help those who might want to try a search on their own to get started; but you will *definitely need to have access to a computer.*

The <u>only information</u> I had to start with was a name and an age. The name I already knew, and the age given was an estimate; and again the information would come from our mother's death certificate.

As I have already stated before in my story, the where-abouts of our father at the time of the death of our mother is unknown; and it was our grandmother, Dora May Killen's duty to fill out the death certificate.

There were only two questions in regards to our father, it asked for the husband's name and his age. Our grand-mother put our father's age at thirty-nine, with a <u>question mark</u> after it. She was obviously unsure of his actual age and was guessing, but it provided me with what I needed; some <u>indication</u> as to how old he was.

I presumed she didn't have the age "nailed down", so I arbitrarily both subtracted and added three years to the one given. This then gave me a time frame, age wise, of him being anywhere from thirty-six to forty-two years of age at the time of our mother's death. With this I would try to establish his "birth year". It was February of 1942 when this document was filled out, so I was looking at a range of years from 1900 to 1906, but also considering that he may also have been born in 1899 as 1942 was only a little over a month "old" at the time of our mother's death.

Judy was a great help in this search. She had joined <u>Genealogy.Com</u> but she didn't have a computer at home. She was hoping to do the searching by using the one at her job but soon realized that would be impractical, the amount of time required to do any kind of a meaningful search just wasn't there. She then gave me her user name and password for the account and I took it upon myself to do the searching; that would work, I was now retired and

I certainly had the time. So, she paid for the search and I did the searching.

Every one knows about the U.S. Census, that national population count performed by our government every ten years.

That would be my starting point, and right from the beginning I accepted the likli- hood that it was going to be a monumental task. I knew he had to be in there somewhere, *but where?* What state, what county, what township or city? I saw, however, that I might possibly have one small advantage.

The people of our country in the early 1900's rarely lived very far from their birthplace throughout their entire lives. People did not move as frequently, or very far from the place where they were born, as commonplace as it is in modern times. In fact, their "entire world" seldom went beyond a twenty-five miles radius of where they lived.

Presuming that was the case with our parents, my initial logic was they were both born in Pennsylvania and lived within the radius just spoken of, with Aston Township being the center. I had it pegged right as to the area where they both grew up as children, but I was dead wrong as to where one of them was born, and that one would be our father.

I would commence my search with the 1920 census, with Aston Township as the starting place; after all, it took me no time at all to find "The Killen's", our mother's side of the family which was located there. It seemed to be the reasonable place to start, and I picked this particular census assuming he would still be a minor and living with his parents.

I had a map pinned to a bulletin board over my computer showing each township, city, town, and borough throughout Delaware County. I was determined to find our father even if I had to go through the census of the entire county.

I went through the census, street by street, for the entire township, careful not to overlook anything for fear of passing over the very information I was looking for.

Some of the handwriting on the data sheets was atrocious, and I found myself scrutinizing those pages while employing the use of a magnifying glass. This was becoming a painstaking, time consuming effort, but I pressed on. Maybe, just perhaps, the *next* page.........

It took me many, many hours to go over the recordings for Aston township; and then followed Concord Township, Bethel Township, Boothwyn, Upper Chichester, Lower Chichester, Linwood, Marcus Hook; and so many other places that it would be redundant to continue listing them.

I even went through the census for Prospect Park and Ridley Park. Bill Ling grew up there his entire life. Had he and our father known each other from years past and not just because of the adoption? Did they know each other as kids; did they go to school together? All the angles; I had to try all the angles!

Nothing meaningful came to the surface, absolutely nothing!

I had deliberately put off the city of Chester, saving it for last, and even though I knew I had a lot more "county" to do; I reluctantly started my search there. I thought; this is going to be "a bird", taking much time canvassing all the wards which constituted this industrial center located on the banks of the Delaware river.

I had been working on it for over two weeks, with Carol helping me pore over the material. This woman who has supported me so much would stay up until two or three o'clock in the morning with me, helping me find my father. She would have to get up at seven o'clock and get herself ready to go to work, but there she was, right by my side.

On one particular night, when I was working solo, I decided to just print out the material and not stop to look over each page. I figured this would be the most time efficient way to approach that evenings work; I would look over the individual sheets sometime during the next day.

The next evening, just after dinner, as Carol was walking down the street to see one of our neighbors, I was starting my routine of methodically examining the data collected when I saw it! It was on the very first page of the stack I was about to systematically wade through! I was transfixed, staring with astonishment at what I was looking at. I had found *our father, our grandparents, and an uncle!*

There listed in the 2nd Ward of the Chester census for 1920 was the street address of 1103 Upland Avenue and its occupants.

They were: Alfred J. Hall, age 38, Head (of household).

Estelle Hall, age 33, wife.

Eugene C. Hall, age 16, son.

Eric W. Hall , age 14, son. And all the members of the household were recorded as being born in *Virginia!*

Census data is not compiled for the year of that census; in other words, the 1920 census does not include information on people for that year. The information recorded is for the ten year span from the year 1910 through 1919. Another example would be for Judy and I; we were born in 1940 and will not be included in that census along with our parents. We won't show up in the census until the one that was taken in 1950, encompassing the years 1940 through 1949.

This new information proved to show that indeed our grandmother Killen was correct in her guess as to our father's age; establishing that he was born in 1903.

My next step in this quest for more family information was writing to the Social Security Administration, and for a nominal fee, acquire a copy pf his *application* for a social security number. I had the basic information I needed, his full name, his parents name, year of birth, and state where he was born. I also identified myself as Eugene C. Hall, Jr.; which by bloodline, I AM! I saw no deception there on my part.

Then I waited.

The document I had requested came after about three week's time. In addition to the information I already knew, it revealed his full date of birth, January 30, 1903, and the actual place of his birth (Heathsville, Virginia); just two more bits of info that would beget more.

It was now time to contact the Bureau of Vital Statistics for the State of Virginia in order to obtain a copy of his birth certificate. That document would prove to be the most valuable of all.

Official records from many states, which includes Virginia, are much more difficult now to obtain since our country was assaulted by terrorists on that day now commonly referred to as 9/11. Understandably, it now entails a very positive identification process to establish the identity of the one requesting the information, and the purpose for which they intend to use that information. And, since the state of Virginia requires a photo I.D. of <u>anyone </u>asking for <u>any</u> legal documents from them, I was now concerned that perhaps my search was about to come to an end.

I didn't know how my Delaware's driver's license, with my photo and the name identifying me as Eugene Ling on it; who was now asking for a birth certificate of a Eugene Carroll Hall, was going to convince the authorities at the Virginia bureau of Vital Statistics that mine was a legitimate inquiry. But I would try anyway, and I took my best shot.

I decided to send along with my request a brief explanation of who I was, Eugene Carroll Hall Jr., and that the name Ling was my adopted name, and included that all important letter mom-mom had sent to Crozer Hospital asking for the names of our parents. I think it was that letter that gave the credibility as to who I was; the post mark from August 1945 would have been incredibly difficult to fabricate.

What astounded me most about the copy of our father's birth certificate was the fact that he apparently, for whatever reason, had requested a copy for himself while living in Pennsylvania. The document I had asked for had *his* *signature* on it!

Excited, I hurriedly looked for my folder containing the info I had compiled on the "Halls." I was frantically searching for it to compare his signature with the one on the _adoption papers!_ THEY WERE THE SAME! It was a positive identification, and I was ecstatic!

I now knew without a doubt I had found the right person. The only remaining question now was what happened to him? Where was he?

It was time now to return to the Genealogy.com site and canvass the Social Security records to find out how many Eugene "Halls" there were. There must have been at least a hundred of them, but only *six* that were born in 1903!

The information gleaned by that knowledge would reveal what states their social security numbers were issued in.

There were two in Connecticut, two in North Carolina, one in Texas, and one in Pennsylvania. It wasn't difficult to figure out which one would be the first to pursue, and I then examined the data from the Social Security Death Index (SSDI) portion of the website. This was the easiest of all the searching I had done, and reasonable to search there. It was now 2002, and if he were still alive he would be ninety-nine years old! Men, at least none that I know of, don't get to live that old!

The information revealed not only his "Social", but also the date of his death and the location at which his last payments were sent to. I now had the location where he had lived the remaining years of his life, South Daytona Beach, Florida.

The next two and final steps in my search was to get an obituary for him from the local newspaper, and his death certificate from the state. I was to be absolutely <u>astonished</u>, <u>flabbergasted</u>, at one piece of information on that document!

His occupation was listed as a *laboratory technician, DuPont Co., Wilmington, DE!* "Like father, like son", my father and I both had worked at the same occupation, for the same company, and a good likelihood at the same site. It is generally believed and accepted that approximately eighty percent of all the technician staff employed by the DuPont Company in the Wilmington area works at the Experimental Station.

There would be one last piece of information on his death certificate that would be beneficial to me. That was the name of his place of burial, and the funeral home that had handled his funeral.

Gary has been in touch with the funeral director and has been able to get the location of Judy and my father's grave. Carol and I plan to visit with Gary in the Spring of 2006, in part to be with him to celebrate his birthday. Also discussed and to be included in our plans is a day trip from the Tampa area over to South Daytona Beach to visit our father's gravesite.

I suspect it will give me final closure to this saga; this long and unique meandering course through time and events that has essentially been my life, and a story that is exclusively mine.

CHAPTER FOURTEEN

CONCLUSION

This book has been the result of much prayer and encouragement.

Prayer on my part, and others; and encouragement from a host of people, most notably my wife.

On many occasions, after she returned home from work, Carol would ask me, "Did you do any writing today?" More than a few times I would reply, "No, I just didn't feel up to it." Her response, and prodding, would be, "Well, get with it 'Ling'; I can't wait to read the finished work!" There were other times when her inspiration for me was something of a chant, something like, "Write, write, write!" She sounded like a cheerleader.

Mike, our eldest son, has also been there for me. Whenever I have been apprehensive about my ability to undertake this project he has been there to encourage me to move forward. He would say, "Just write it, Dad." "Don't worry about the spelling, grammar and such, deal with that later." And, he has also told me several times, "You need to call Oprah!"

I have not done that, as I honestly believe my story is more about the Lord than it is of me.

My reluctance to write was centered on the realization that in order for this story to "work", I would have to get _very_ personal and candidly honest; perhaps share some things that were borderline embarrassing, something I wasn't sure I wanted to do.

But while thinking on this, it was then that I began to focus on my _real_ goal; which was to give my testimony as to how the Lord has worked in my life. Without question, my life has been a very vivid and obvious demonstration of his sovereignty; and my story has been an excellent opportunity for me to offer a personal testimony of my salvation experience.

But even after so many people had encouraged me to put my story down on paper, I was still very apprehensive. As a result, I felt a real need for some _conclusive_ indication from the Lord that it was something _HE_ wanted me to do; so I started to methodically and fervently pray about it.

Ultimately my answer was to come from two sources, my pastor and my sister.

I made an appointment with our pastor, the Rev. Matt Mancini, to discuss what my intent was, and see what his thoughts were on the idea.

After explaining what it was I wanted to do, he asked me, "What is it you want to accomplish by writing this book?" My answer was automatic and direct, "I am hoping to share how the Lord has worked in my life, and hopefully it will be a testimony, and perhaps lead someone to Christ. If it should reach only one person, then it will be worth it." He then smiled and said, "That's a no-brainer." He continued to explain, "If your intention is to bring Glory to God, and witness for Christ, then you can be sure you have the leading of the Holy Spirit."

What an encouragement!

Still, me *being me*, I wasn't sure. I had never written anything before, except some poetry, and I continued to question my ability. However, it would not be very long after that meeting that the Lord would "speak to me" once again.

It was during a visit Judy and I had made to our mother's gravesite at Lawncroft.

We had placed some flowers on her grave, had prayer, shed a few tears (as we always seem to do) and were now on our way back to our cars when she said to me, "It seems to me that He (God) wants us to know; and I get the feeling that *we're supposed to do something."*

It were these remarks that made me decide to move forward, and I truly believe these two exchanges were the "confirmations" I had been looking for. I decided, then and there, that I would pursue what I believed the Lord wanted me to do.

So, with that in mind, my reasons for writing this book has been, to a limited extent, an opportunity to share Judy's and my life's story; a story we believe to be a fascinating one.

But most importantly, it has been an appropriate occasion in which to share the obvious evidence of God's sovereignty working throughout my life, and to give witness to the working of the Holy Spirit to bring me to Christ.

And, in addition, to give encouragement to those who are adopted, especially to the abused, to let them know that God has not forgotten them, whatever their situation; and to let them know their only hope for a truly full and productive life lies in a relationship with God, and can only come from a personal faith in Jesus Christ.

And, after reflecting on the Lord's leading, and Judy's statement; it is, I believe, part of *His purpose for me.*

> All the days ordained for me were written in your book before one of them came to be.
>
> —Psalm 139:16 (NIV)

ADDENDUM

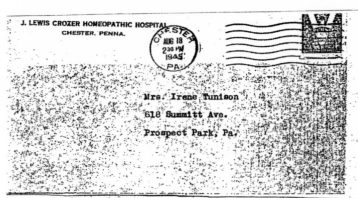

J. LEWIS CROZER HOMEOPATHIC HOSPITAL
CHESTER, PA.

August 18th, 1945

Mrs. Irene Tunison
618 Summitt Ave.
Prospect Park, Pa.

Dear Madam:-

From the records of this Hospital I find that:-

Eugene Carroll Hall, Jr and Judith Lee Hall were born in J. Lewis Crozer Hospital Chester, Pa. on Jan. 16, 1940. The father's name was Eugene Carroll Hall and the mother Theodora Estelle Killem(Maiden name).

This is information desired, I believe.

Yours very truly,

Jerome L. Benzing

Jerome L. Benzing
Superintendent

The letter that started it all.

250

COUNTY OF DELAWARE
DEPARTMENT OF HUMAN SERVICES

CWLA
Child Welfare
League of America
Member Agency

OFFICE OF
CHILDREN & YOUTH SERVICES

Council

Wallace H. Nunn
Chairman

John J. McFadden
Vice Chairman

Kathrynann W. Durham
Tim Murtaugh
Andrew J. Reilly

May 9, 2001

John F. Bauer, Director
Department of Human Services

Mary Germond, M.S.W., L.S.W.
Office of Children and Youth

Mr. Eugene Ling
5 Hardy Rd.
New Castle, DE 19720

Dear Mr. Ling,

Enclosed you will find the final Decree from your adoption that occurred in April of 1942. As previously discussed there was very little information in your Orphan's Court File. Because you did have the identifying information regarding your birthfather and it states in the court work that your birth mother is deceased, I have opted to give you this information without whiting out anything.

Regrettably, I am unable to give you more information at this time regarding your birth family. I will send a letter to Social Security today to see if they have any information. Social Security can take some time. The response time varies from two to six months depending on the demand. I do not have birth dates or former addresses for your birth family so it may take a little longer.

Once you review the information you may find information missing (This was my initial impression at least most of the court documents are only signature pages). I am also speculating that your adoptive family may have known your birth family because there was no Intermediary in your court documents.

I will do my best to assist you with your search for more information. If you have questions regarding your search feel free to contact me at the number listed below.

Sincerely,

Tamika Q. Wayne

Tamika Wayne, BSW
Adoption Search Caseworker

UPPER DARBY OFFICE
20 South 69th Street, 3rd Floor
Upper Darby, Pa 19082
(610) 713-2000
FAX (610) 713-2340

CHESTER OFFICE
531 Penn Street
Chester, Pa 19013
(610) 447-1000
Fax (610) 447-1016

LEGAL SERVICES DEPARTMENT
Government Center, Room 130
201 West Front Street
Media, Pa 19063
(610) 891-5104
Fax (610) 891-0489

SEXUAL ABUSE CENTER
100 West 6th Street
Ground Floor
Media, Pa 19063
(610) 891-5258
Fax (610) 891-0481

TOLL FREE NUMBER 1-800-416-4511

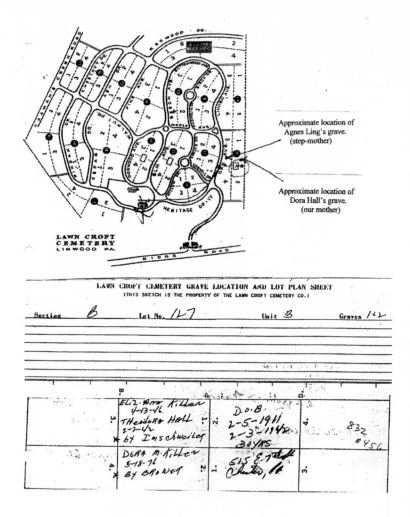

Approximate location of
Agnes Ling's grave.
(step-mother)

Approximate location of
Dora Hall's grave.
(our mother)

LAWN CROFT
CEMETERY
LINWOOD PA.

LAWN CROFT CEMETERY GRAVE LOCATION AND LOT PLAN SHEET
(THIS SKETCH IS THE PROPERTY OF THE LAWN CROFT CEMETERY CO.)

Section _B_   Lot No. _127_   Unit _B_   Graves _1 & 2_

	Eliz. Ann Killen 4-13-46 3. Theodora Hall 1-7-42 ✱ by Imschweiler	D.O.B. 2-5-1911 2-3-1942 30 yrs	832 056
	Dora M. Killen 3-18-76 ✱ By Brower	515 E. 7th Chester, PA	

1798962   **COMMONWEALTH OF VIRGINIA**
DEPARTMENT OF HEALTH – DIVISION OF VITAL RECORDS

COMMONWEALTH OF VIRGINIA
DEPARTMENT OF HEALTH—BUREAU OF VITAL STATISTICS
DELAYED CERTIFICATE OF BIRTH

13514

1. Place of Birth
City or County __Northumberland__   Street No. or Post office __Rainswood,__
2. Full name of child __EUGENE CARROLL HALL,__   Soc. Security Number
3. Sex of child __Male__   4. Were parents married to each other? __YES__   5. Date of child's birth __January 9th 1903__
(Month by name) (Day) (Year)

FATHER OF CHILD	MOTHER OF CHILD
6. Full name __Alfred Julius Hall__	10. Full maiden name __Rene Estelle Welsh__
7. Color or race __White__ 8. Age at time of this birth __21__ Yrs.	11. Color or race __White__ 12. Age at time of this birth __17__ Yrs.
9. Birthplace __Richmond County, Virginia.__	13. Birthplace __Richmond County, Virginia.__

Certification of Attending Physician, Parent, or an Other Relative Who Was Nearby. I hereby certify that the above statements are correct:
Sign here __Alfred J. Hall__   Present address __Chester, Del. Co., Penna.__
(Only Notary Public may witness if by X)

City of
I, Notary Public of County of __Chester, Del. Co.,__ State of __Pennsylvania,__
do attest that the above certificate of birth was signed in my presence by __Alfred Julius Hall,__
who declares under oath that the statements made above and known to be so because of relationship as: __FATHER__ Age of person signing: __60__ A family Bible examined by me, printed in the year __1900__, contains an unaltered record apparently made near the time, showing the birth of __Eugene Carroll Hall,__ on (date) __Jan. 30th 1903.__
Other evidence or comments

Date __May 8th__ 19 __42__   Attest: __J. Albert Northam.__
My commission expires __1-1-'46__ 19   Notary Public
Do not use rubber stamp.   Affix-seal above this line.

Applicant's Signature __Eugene C. Hall__   Mailing address __2801 West Third Street,__
(If practical). Sign exactly as accustomed to do at present—for identification and mailing.   __Chester, Del. Co., Pa.__

Abstract of written evidence submitted to the Bureau of Vital Statistics.

Date of Filing __May 11. 1942__   State Registrar

I, Eugene Hall, the father of Judith Hall and Eugen
hereby certify that I have acknowledged to be the father o
said minor children, that I have read the foregoing Petiti
that the facts set forth therein are true and correct, and
join in the prayer thereof and do consent to the adoption
Judith Hall and Eugene Hall by William T. Ling and Elizab
Ling.

__Eugene H__

Comparison of signatures to confirm that we had indeed found the right person, our biological father, Eugene C. Hall.
The first document is a request that he made (for whatever reason) for a copy of his own birth certificate. The bottom document is from the adoption decree. They match!

253

Finders Keepers

For information on our search group,
please contact Ginger Farrow at:
SearchDE@aol.com.

For those without access to a computer
please write to:

Finders Keepers

P.O. Box 181, Bear, Delaware, 19701-0181

The author may be reached at
ling1940@aol.com

Printed in the United States
65666LVS00002B

9 781414 107264